Battleground Marlborough

BLENHEID
1704

MARLBOROUGH'S GREATEST VICTORY

Brian Gallagher
Madera
HP8 4SN
01494 767891
1.9.04

With the continued expansion of the Battleground series a **Battleground Series Club** has been formed to benefit the reader. The purpose of the Club is to keep members informed of new titles and to offer many other reader-benefits. Membership is free and by registering an interest you can help us predict print runs and thus assist us in maintaining the quality and prices at their present levels.

Please call the office 01226 734555, or send your name and address along with a request for more information to:
Battleground Series Club Pen & Sword Books Ltd,
47 Church Street, Barnsley, South Yorkshire S70 2AS

Battleground Marlborough

BLENHEIM
1704

MARLBOROUGH'S GREATEST VICTORY

James Falkner

Pen & Sword
MILITARY

For Myra with love

First published in Great Britain in 2004 by
Pen & Sword Military
an imprint of
Pen & Sword Books Ltd
47 Church Street
Barnsley
South Yorkshire
S70 2AS

Copyright © James Falkner 2004

ISBN 1-84415-050-X

The right of James Falkner to be identified as Author of the Work
has been asserted by him in accordance with the Copyright, Designs and
Patents Act 1988.

A CIP catalogue record for this book is
available from the British Library

Typeset in Century Old Style

Printed and bound in Great Britain by CPI UK

For a complete list of Pen & Sword titles, please contact
Pen & Sword Books Limited
47 Church Street, Barnsley, South Yorkshire, S70 2AS, England
E-mail: enquiries@pen-and-sword.co.uk
Website: www.pen-and-sword.co.uk

CONTENTS

Blindheim village under attack. British infantry in the foreground.

Introduction

ON 13 AUGUST 1704, during the War of the Spanish Succession, Queen Anne's Captain-General led his troops to a stunning victory over a larger French and Bavarian army on the banks of the River Danube. The Englishman was John Churchill, 1st Duke of Marlborough, his army was drawn from Britain, Holland, the Protestant German states, Denmark and Imperial Austria, and the battle was at Blenheim on the northern borders of Bavaria.

England (Great Britain from 1707) became a world power that day in 1704, with an extraordinary extension of her reach and influence. This can still be seen today, as the United Kingdom still 'punches above its weight' on the international scene; such has been the case ever since 1704. The battle beside the Danube was the acknowledged wonder of the age, and men wrote afterwards that the news from southern Germany was so exciting that it was impossible to sleep. The Virginian rake, Colonel Parke, had galloped into London town a week or so after the battle, with a scrap of paper in his hand, announcing to the Queen the triumph over France and her allies. Not until the arrival of the Waterloo Despatch in 1815 would such scenes be witnessed again in those streets. Marlborough was acclaimed as the foremost captain of his generation, and a grateful monarch and nation endowed the Duke with enough money to build a great palace at Woodstock in Oxfordshire, suitable and fit for such a hero. Appropriately enough, that palace was to be known as Blenheim Palace, and it is now the home of His Grace the 11th Duke of Marlborough.

All the war aims of King Louis XIV of France were ruined that August day in 1704. The previous fifty or so years had witnessed a series of aggressive campaigns waged upon his unlucky neighbours and French territorial expansion, into southern Flanders, Artois, Picardy, Languedoc, Lorraine and Alsace, had carried that nation to her present-day borders, more or less. Louis XIV was an accomplished soldier, and when a young man had enjoyed being on campaign. However, the success of French arms had largely been the result of the labours of the great Marshals of France of that time – Condé, Turenne, Vauban, Luxembourg and others. Over the years, the French had acquired a glorious tradition of victory. At Blenheim Marlborough led his soldiers, brought from the Low Countries to Bavaria by a deception played on both his own Parliament and the Dutch States-General, to a crushing victory over an entire French army. Thousands of prisoners and horses, scores of senior officers, regimental colours, cavalry standards, and guns, all fell into his hands, while a French Marshal sat captive, sipping chocolate in the Duke's own coach. The destruction in the field of an entire army of the Sun King was a thing unknown in the memories of living men. The shock and disbelief this produced across Europe, the effect upon carefully crafted alliances, and the adulation that it brought to Marlborough as the victor, cannot be overstated. That the campaign was of the most daring kind, and the successful result finely balanced, adds to the fascination of the story.

The great contest at Blenheim took place on a battlefield that stretches for nearly four miles northwards from the Danube river to the Swabian hills. The battle is named after Blindheim (Blenheim) village, but is often known in France and Germany as the Battle of Höchstädt 1704 (not the lesser fight there in September 1703 which the French won). There has been little intrusive modern development of the site, although in the nineteenth century a railway line was put through the area, on the same general axis as the main road from Ulm to Donauwörth. Still, the wide Bavarian cornfields, small copses of trees and the bordering heavily wooded hills are all very attractive. So too are the small pretty villages – Blindheim, Oberglau, Unterglau and Lutzingen – each with their distinctive church tower, around which brutal infantry battles raged in the summer of 1704. These places are somewhat larger now, and the houses are smarter and larger than of old. Despite this, the general feel of the villages and farms has apparently not changed greatly, and the visitor to this beautiful area today can visualise the awful and dramatic contest of 300 years ago, without too great an effort of imagination.

Note on Old and New Styles of dating

In the early eighteenth century the Julian calendar (Old Style or O.S.) was still in use in the British Isles, whereas on the Continent the Gregorian calendar (New Style or N.S.) was used. This system was 10 days ahead of the old, up to 1700, and 11 days ahead thereafter. As Britain adopted the Gregorian calendar later in the eighteenth century, and almost all the narrative takes place on the Continent, I have used New Style throughout this book, unless indicated otherwise.

Spelling and grammar

I have not altered the original, often rather idiosyncratic, spelling found in many of the contemporary quotations. Where others have already put the grammar into modern form, no attempt has been made to change this.

British, Dutch and German troops, and others

In 1704 the English, Scots and Irish armies each had their own separate establishment and budget (many Welsh soldiers served, of course, but there was no separate Welsh establishment). Contemporary accounts often refer to all these troops as being 'English', but I have used the more precise term where appropriate, as in 'a Scottish battalion.' Although the term 'British' was not really in use until after the 1707 Act of Union, I have occasionally referred to Queen Anne's soldiers, *en bloc*, as being 'British' to avoid having to use unduly lengthy phrases such as 'English, Scots and Irish troops.' To complicate matters, the Dutch recruited numbers of Scottish regiments into their service, but few of these were engaged in the 1704 Danube campaign.

In a similar fashion, the States-General of Holland also employed large numbers of German and Protestant Swiss troops. As these were paid and clothed by the Dutch, they are usually referred to as 'Dutch' troops. Many German units from princely states owing allegiance to the Emperor in Vienna are referred to as 'Imperial' troops even though they were not Austrian.

France also had substantial contingents of foreign troops in her army, the Swiss and émigré Irish being among the most notable. In addition, Tallard's forces on the Danube were bolstered by a number of Walloon regiments (sometimes, confusingly, referred to as 'Spanish' troops – being from the Spanish Netherlands.)

The day the battle was fought

Even such monumental works as Frank Taylor's *Wars of Marlbrough* (1921) and Winston Churchill's *Marlborough, His Life and Times* (1933) appear not to comment on the day of the week that Blenheim was fought. Charles MacFarlane, in his *Life of Marlborough* (1854), says, however, that 'As early as two o'clock in the morning of Sunday, the memorable 13 August' the Allied army began its march onto the battlefield; and Virginia Cowles in her *The Great Marlborough and His Duchess* (1983) wrote that the Allied troops heard Divine Service under French artillery fire 'as it was Sunday morning.' I have hitherto followed this same line, but reference to the calendar for 1706, when the battle of Ramillies was undoubtedly fought on Whit Sunday, 23 May, shows plainly that 13 August in that year was a Friday. If this is so, then the same date in 1704 must be a Wednesday, not Sunday (neither 1705 or 1706 were leap years, so there is no complication from that quarter to take into account). Furthermore, a bulletin issued from the Allied camp on 17 August 1704 speaks of 'Our army, which lay on their arms in the enemy's camp on Wednesday night after the battle.' Contemporary documents are powerful evidence, but they are not infallible – clerical or later printing errors are not uncommon, so corroboration was sought, and found, in William Coxe's *Memoirs of John, Duke of Marlborough* (1848). On page 99, a letter written by a French officer immediately after the action is given, which includes the line: *'Je vous dirai que Mercredi 13 Aout il s'en donne la plus sanglante bataille qu'on ait vue de memoire d'homme, et dans laquelle nous avons été entièrement defaits. M. Tallard est blessé.'* So, it seems that it was Wednesday.

Glossary

Battalion	Basic infantry unit. About 650 men strong in the Allied armies.
Brigade	Tactical grouping of battalions (called regiments in some armies).
Canister (shot)	Cans of musket balls fired from a cannon (cartouche/partridge).
Carbine	A shortened musket used by cavalry and dragoons.
Cuirassiers	Armoured cavalry. Rather outdated by 1704.
Defile	A narrow pass or opening, relatively easy to defend.
Dragoons	Mounted infantry, often used as cavalry.
Enfilade	To take in the flank, by fire or movement.
Fascines	Bundles of sticks, used to fill ditches, trenches and holes.
Gabion	Wicker basket filled with earth, used to make instant defences.
Generall (the)	Drum roll, calling soldiers to form in their ranks.
Grenade	Cast-iron bomb, thrown by grenadiers.
Grenadier	Tall soldier, armed with grenades and hatchet, as well as musket.
Hanger	Cheap sword, carried by infantrymen.
Howitzer	Short barrelled field gun, fired at high trajectory.
Picquets	Outposts, both cavalry and infantry.
Pioneers	Soldiers and conscripted peasants who cleared away obstacles.
Platoon	Basic infantry sub-unit. Usually about 35 men strong.
Pontoons	Temporary bridges made of boats.
Roundshot	Cannon balls.
Troop	Basic cavalry sub-unit. About 80 men strong in the Allied army.
Wing	Half of an army, left or right. Equivalent to modern army corps.

Chapter 1

THE WAR FOR SPAIN

O N 1 NOVEMBER 1700 the crippled and feeble-minded King Carlos II of Spain died in Madrid. He had been described as more a medical curiosity than a man, and he had no children. Carlos was for some time susceptible to French influence at his court and, despite carefully agreed international treaties on the matter of the succession, in his will he left the throne of Spain to Philippe, Duc d'Anjou, the youngest grandson of King Louis XIV of France, the Sun King.

The news of the death of the King of Spain came to the French court at Fontainebleau on 9 November 1700 and, despite the excitement that this caused, Louis XIV was at first reluctant to allow Anjou to accept. The intention to bestow the crown on the French prince had been known for some time, but now it was a fact the likely implications had to be faced. Two Partition Treaties, negotiated in the late 1690s, had brought to a tired end the seemingly interminable French-Dutch wars of the last century, and they set out, among other things, that the crowns of France and Spain should always be kept separate. Such a new development as this inheritance, with a French prince on the Spanish throne,

King Charles (Carlos) II of Spain, died 1 November 1700. 'More a medical curiosity than a man.'

must put this important provision in doubt. Not only was Catholic France the single most populous country in Western Europe, she was militarily the most powerful. Louis XIV had a long history of aggressive territorial expansion at the expense of her near neighbours. To ally the military power of France with the vast Spanish Empire in the Mediterranean and the Americas would alarm every Protestant prince in Europe, and war might result. The French king had achieved much, but he was ageing and, with

Phillippe, Duc d'Anjou, King Philip V of Spain, the French claimant. He was the grandson of Louis XIV.

his treasury in a sorry state, another war was not at all what he wished for.

Despite the dangers, Louis XIV reluctantly allowed Anjou to accept the Spanish throne, and the new king, now Philip V of Spain, was introduced to the Spanish Ambassador, Castel del Rey, on 16 November 1700. The Duc de St Simon, who witnessed the glittering scene, wrote:

> *Contrary to all precedent, the King caused the double doors of his cabinet* [private suite] *to be thrown open and ordered all the crowd assembled without to enter. Glancing majestically over the numerous company, 'Gentlemen' said he, indicating the Duc d'Anjou, 'This is the King of Spain.'*

Soon afterwards, Anjou and a glittering entourage left for Madrid. However, Austria also had a claimant to the throne, the Archduke Charles, son of Emperor Leopold. Louis XIV moved quickly to avert conflict and messages were sent to Vienna, London and the Dutch States-General in the Hague, giving assurances that the French and Spanish thrones would always be kept separate, and that the interests of all those neighbouring states would not be put at risk by this inheritance. All might have been well, for French diplomatic activity was intense, and important territorial concessions in northern Italy were offered to Austria. Unexpectedly Louis XIV, usually so adroit, now fumbled the diplomatic scene.

Anxious to protect his grandson's inheritance in the Spanish Netherlands (present-day Belgium), in February 1701 Louis XIV sent French troops to seize a string of strategically important towns (Luxembourg, Namur, Mons,

Louis XIV, the 'Sun King'. His miscalculation over the throne of Spain brought war back to Europe.

13

Charleroi, Oudenarde, Maastricht, Ath and Nieuport). These fortresses constituted a cherished barrier for the Dutch against renewed French aggression, but the Governor-General in the Spanish Netherlands, Maximilien-Emmanuel Wittelsbach, the Elector of Bavaria, unwisely connived at the French operation and the Dutch were caught off guard. Their garrisons were humiliatingly interned by Marshal Boufflers, the French commander, and only Maastricht, whose Dutch governor seemed particularly robust, was saved. Although William III of England (and Dutch Stadtholder) was informed in advance of this move, by the French Ambassador in London, Camille d'Hostun, Duc de Tallard, he kept the information to himself and the Dutch States-General understandably took alarm at the loss of the towns. Matters were made worse when, in September 1701, Louis XIV went to St Germain and stood at the deathbed of James II, the exiled King of England, and acknowledged to his dying friend that his own son, the Chevalier de St George, was considered by France to be the rightful heir to the English throne. This again abrogated the Partition Treaties and gave great offence in London when it became known. Tallard, the French Ambassador, was expelled from England.

Increasingly, the threat from France to its neighbours appeared to grow more acute, and earnest negotiations took place between William III, the States-General and the Austrian Emperor Leopold, to form an alliance to limit the power of Louis XIV. A Treaty of Grand Alliance was concluded on 7 September 1701, but William III did not live to see another war. On 19 March 1702 he died from the effects of a fall from his horse a couple of weeks earlier. His sister-in-law, the Princess Anne, youngest daughter of James II, ascended the English throne. Despite this change on the throne in London the rather nervous Dutch were reassured as to England's sincerity. War was declared on France on 15 May 1702, at the gates of St James's Palace in London, and simultaneously in the Hague and Vienna. On hearing the news, Louis XIV remarked drily 'I must be growing old if ladies are now declaring war on me.'

The French had not been idle during the preceding months, and Louis XIV raised 100 new regiments at this time (some units were of dubious quality, such was the haste to augment the army). On learning of the declaration of war, the immediate French response was to mount a campaign against the Dutch. Two armies were ready for this, both under the nominal command of

Louis XIV invites Castel del Rey, the Spanish envoy, to greet his new King, Philip V, in November 1700.

the King's grandson and heir, the Duc de Bourgogne. The Marquis de Bedmar commanded the 'Spanish' Walloon and Flemish troops near Brussels, while Marshal Boufflers had a 60,000-strong French army ready to advance into southern Holland from Brabant. The Dutch field commander, Rodert van Ginkel, Earl Athlone, was an energetic commander but he was outmanoeuvred and soon found his army (mostly Dutch, and those in Dutch pay, but also with the British troops so far assembled for the campaign) pinned against the lower Maas river near to Clèves. Had Boufflers not over-extended his lines of supply from Brabant, the French campaign might have been rapidly successful, and the Dutch driven right out of the war. That would end the Grand Alliance neatly and Philip V would be King of Spain without further ado.

However, the Allied forces steadily gathering in the Low Countries were nearly 60,000 strong when John Churchill, the fifty-two year-old Earl of Marlborough, was appointed as field commander of the Anglo-Dutch armies (but only when on campaign). Delayed by diplomatic business in London and the

John Churchill, 1st Duke of Marlborough

John Churchill was born in Devon in 1650. His family were impoverished by the English Civil War but his father's connections secured the young man a place at the court of King Charles II at the Restoration. Having entered the army, Churchill served in Tangier, and on attachment to the French army, in one of the English regiments loaned to King Louis XIV for the latest of his wars with the Dutch. Churchill was introduced to the Sun King while on campaign at this time, and also met many of the French officers he would fight and defeat many years later.

Churchill commanded the royal infantry at Sedgemoor in 1685 when the Monmouth Rebellion came to grief, but he defected from James II to William of Orange in 1688. Despite this the Dutch king did not trust Churchill, who spent some time in the Tower of London on flimsy charges of treason, before being restored to royal favour. His influence grew steadily, and he helped William III negotiate the Treaty of Grand Alliance with the States-General of Holland and Imperial Austria. When Queen Anne came to the throne in 1702, Earl Marlborough (as he had become) and his wife Sarah were her best and most loved friends. Appointed Captain-General of Land Forces, Marlborough campaigned with success in the Low Countries, and was made a duke for his services, before taking his army to the Danube in the campaign that led to Blenheim in August 1704. This triumph marked the duke as the greatest captain of his age.

The following year Marlborough led the Anglo-Dutch army to a stunning victory at Elixheim to the south-east of Brussels. Having decoyed the French commander, Marshal Villeroi, southwards towards Namur, Marlborough carried out a rapid night march to break through the defensive Lines of Brabant with his British, Danish and German troops. They were almost immediately ferociously attacked by a French and Bavarian corps under Count
Caraman and the Marquis d'Alègre. Marlborough was well forward, fighting hand to hand in the swirling cavalry action, and a Bavarian horse-grenadier almost sabred him. The stroke went wide when the soldier lost his balance and fell to the ground, where the Duke's trumpeter killed him. Such typical gallantry in the Duke, with his life at as much risk as the humblest soldier, endeared him to his men, who knew him as 'the Old Corporal' – the one who led them, fed them, and ensured they were paid. There is no greater compliment for a general.

To the successes at Blenheim and Elixheim the Duke subsequently added victories at Ramillies (1706), where he was thrown from his horse and almost ridden down by French cavalry, and Oudenarde (1708). He then laid siege to and captured France's second city, Lille, which fell to his army in December 1708. Despite such successes the war for Spain dragged on, and the bitter-sweet victory at Malplaquet in September 1709, where Marlborough's losses were nearly twice those of the French, added to his failing influence. He was dismissed from all his posts in December 1711. Concerned at politically motivated charges of embezzlement of public funds, the Duke went to live abroad with the Duchess. He returned to London on the accession of George I to the English throne in 1714. Restored to his appointments by the German king, Marlborough suffered increasingly ill health, and died at Windsor Lodge in June 1722.

Hague, he arrived to take command early in June 1702. Although Ginkel was inclined to be uncooperative, Marlborough took firm control of the operations, using to good advantage the temporary pause in the French campaign brought on by lack of supplies. 'This superb commander' as Ginkel grudgingly, but admiringly, called the Englishman, marched south and westwards towards Liège on 26 July 1702. The move threatened the French lines of supply and communication and forced Boufflers to withdraw into Brabant. Marlborough could have mauled the disordered French army as it withdrew across the Heaths of Peer, had the Dutch been inclined to involve their troops in a battle at that place. They thought it too risky, and the Earl had to watch his opponents hurry past 'in the greatest disorder imaginable' and out of his reach.

Archduke Charles of Austria, King Charles III of Spain, the Austrian claimant. He subsequently became Emperor Charles of Austria.

This set the pattern for campaigns over the next eighteen months. Marlborough (soon made a duke as reward for his successes in the Low Countries) would march out to challenge the French armies, only to have the cautious Dutch field deputies decide that the conditions were not right and refuse permission to engage in pitched battle. This attitude may be understood, for a defeat in battle would lay their frontier open to French invasion, while England was sheltered by the Channel. Still, the Duke's hopes of a decisive victory, with the French field army defeated and in flight, were frustrated by Dutch caution, whatever the reasons for that might be.

Chapter 2

A STOLEN ARMY

HE DUKE of Marlborough's difficulties with the Dutch persisted through 1703, although his army did manage to seize a number of French-held fortresses in the Spanish Netherlands. The States-General minted a medal in the Duke's honour, inscribed 'Victorious without Slaughter.' However, Marlborough could see that this was no way to win a war against the French. Eager to get away from the restraining and cautious hands of the Dutch field deputies, who could effectively veto his plans if they seemed to be too risky, the Duke devised a plan with the Imperial Austrian Ambassador in London, Count Wratislaw, to take his army to southern Germany. The Elector of Bavaria, although nominally owing allegiance to the Austrian Emperor, had concluded an alliance with Louis XIV, partly to safeguard his role as Governor-General in the Spanish Netherlands, but also to take advantage of Vienna's present weakness. The Imperial armies, having to contend with rebellion in Hungary and campaigns on the Upper Rhine, the Tyrol and in Italy, were losing the war with the French and their Bavarian allies; Vienna was under threat, and if it fell then so too would the Grand Alliance.

Queen Anne of Great Britain. She sent Marlborough to the Danube.

Queen Anne gave Marlborough an order to go to the aid of Austria 'if he saw fit', and on 19 April 1704 the Duke crossed from Harwich to Holland. He wrote from the Hague to a friend in London on 29 April:

My intentions are to march with all the English [troops in English pay] *to Coblenz and to declare that I*

18

intend to campaign on the Moselle; but when I come there, to
write to the [Dutch] States that I think it absolutely necessary
for the saving of the Empire to march with the troops under my
command and to join with those that are in Germany in order
to take measures with Prince Louis of Baden [the Imperial
Field Commander] *for the speedy reduction of the Elector of*
Bavaria.

The Dutch, whose worry remained the security of their southern
borders, were reluctant to see the Captain-General march away,
and even planned to recall some of the troops in their pay that had
been serving on the Upper Rhine. They were persuaded to agree
to the new campaign, for Marlborough made it plain that he
intended to march southwards with or without their blessing, and
he convinced them that his intention was really a campaign
against the Marquis de Bedmar in the Moselle valley. During
discussions early in May, the Duke assured the Dutch that he
would return in good time if the French commander in the
Spanish Netherlands, Marshal Villeroi, mounted an attack on
Holland. In fact, Marlborough had calculated that, as he marched
south, taking the course of the Rhine, the French commander
would be drawn after him, to avoid being outflanked, with no time
or leisure to attack the Dutch. In the event this was proved to be
the case.

On 4 May 1704 the British garrison at Breda began moving to
the concentration area ordered by Marlborough. Other garrisons
joined the march, and Marlborough's younger brother, General
Charles Churchill, took command of the troops on 8 May. The
river Meuse was crossed at Ruremond on 14 May, and a few days
later the concentration area at Bedburg near Cologne was
reached. After a grand review of the army, on 19 May 1704
Marlborough's troops began their march southwards from
Bedburg. The Duke's route, which at first was along the west
bank of the Rhine, was clear only because of his successes in the
previous two years in clearing out the French garrisons from the
towns past which he now marched. The pace that the Duke set
was not severe: exhausted soldiers would be of no use when the
time came to fight, and the arrangements to supply the marching
army were excellent so the troops made good time. Veldt Marshal
Henry of Nassau, Count Overkirk, was left with the Dutch troops
to watch their borders, but he almost immediately took alarm, and
begged the Duke to suspend his operations. Marlborough

reassured him, but declined to do so, for, as he had anticipated, as his army moved southwards the strategic emphasis of the war inexorably moved with it.

While the Allied preparations for the great march had been progressing, the French were striving to maintain Marshal Ferdinand Marsin with his army in Bavaria. The Marshal had been operating with the Elector of Bavaria against the Imperial commander, Prince Louis-Guillaume, Margrave of Baden. Despite local successes, Marsin was rather isolated, and his lines of supply and communication with France lay through the rocky passes of the Black Forest. On 12 May 1704, Marshal Tallard began to take a convoy of supplies, money and troop reinforcements from the Rhine to support Marsin. With considerable skill, he brought the huge, vulnerable column through the difficult country, neatly outmanoeuvring Baron Thüngen, the Imperial

Louis-Guillaume, Margrave of Baden (1655–1707). He commanded Imperial troops at the Schellenberg and was wounded in the foot.

general who sought to block his path. Marsin marched westwards to meet Tallard, and received 8,000 fresh troops, a vast quantity of supplies and munitions, and over one million louis d'or in cash, to sustain his army in Bavaria. Tallard then returned with his own force to the Rhine, once again side-stepping Thüngen's efforts to intercept him. This whole vast operation was an outstanding military achievement, and greatly to Tallard's credit.

In the north, Marshal Villeroi had watched the red-coated soldiers march away in some puzzlement. If they marched south, then it seemed he must follow, and the Dutch borders, as a result, would remain safe. His appeal to Louis XIV for advice met with the dry response 'If the Duke marches, then so too must you march'.

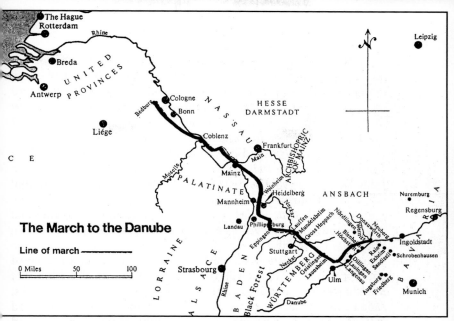

The March to the Danube

Line of march ——————

0 Miles   50   100

As events unfolded, the Dutch saw that Marlborough's assessment of French reaction to his moves was correct, and their fears were calmed. Captain Robert Parker, who tramped up the Rhine with the Royal Irish Regiment, wrote late in May that:

> Villeroi by this time had arrived at Treves with the greater part of his army from the Netherlands, to oppose the Duke in this quarter. This made the Dutch easy, for they were apprehensive, that on the Duke's marching from them, the French would over-run their whole country.

So secure did the States-General feel that Johan Goor, whose Dutch corps had been operating on the Upper Rhine with an Imperial army, was soon informed that he was under Marlborough's orders, should the Duke wish to use him in this new far-off campaign. Meanwhile Marlborough's army marched onwards, and was reinforced at regular intervals by contingents of Hessian, Prussian and Hanoverian troops, which the Duke had arranged should rendezvous with him as he moved towards the south. Sombre news came in, however, for on 23 May Marlborough learned of Tallard's success in reinforcing and replenishing Marsin's army. Such an operation, while a drag on French resources, might well be attempted again, and the next time Tallard and his own army might well remain in Bavaria to confront the Duke.

On 26 May Marlborough's troops reached Coblenz, where the

Moselle river met the Rhine, and huge amounts of stores for the coming campaign had been gathered in advance. If the Duke was going to attack Isidore Bedmar he must now turn to the west into the Moselle valley. Instead, the following day the army crossed to the eastern bank of the Rhine and Captain Blackader, one of Marlborough's marching captains, wrote that

> *This is likely to be a campaign of great fatigue and trouble.*
> *I know not where they are heading us.'*

John Deane, serving with the 1st English Foot Guards, simply wrote in his journal

> *'On the 15th* [O.S.] *marched and incampt by Coblentz.*
> *Here my Lord Duke left us and tooke the horse with him before*
> *us into Germany.'*

The infantry turned to the east across the Rhine on a bridge of pontoon boats. 'There will be no campaign on the Moselle', Marshal Villeroi wrote to Louis XIV as he received reports of the Allied movement, 'the English have all gone up into Germany.' Not the Moselle certainly, but the Duke could still strike at Alsace, for he had his engineers construct a pontoon bridge of boats across the Rhine at Philipsburgh, as if for that very purpose. Meanwhile, Marlborough's army marched steadily onwards. The Elector of Mainz approvingly reviewed the British troops, and the River Neckar at Heidelberg was reached, as the weather worsened and rain turned the roads heavy with mud.

The most careful preparations had been made for the march up the Rhine: the availability of supplies depended upon hard cash, and the ability of the English treasury to pay in gold ensured that frequent stockpiles of food, fodder, boots and clothes awaited the marching soldiers. Local farmers, assured that they would be paid for produce, brought their wares to the roadside to sell to the quartermasters as the army marched past. As Robert Parker remembered approvingly:

> *Surely never was such a march carried on with more order*
> *or regularity and with less fatigue both to man and horse.*

Marlborough's chaplain, Dr Francis Hare, wrote that:

> *His Grace was not unmindful to provide money and order*
> *regular payments for everything that was brought into the*
> *camp, a thing unknown hitherto in Germany.*

Not all went well though, as the weather had turned unseasonably bad, and John Deane wrote:

> *It hath rayned thirty-two days together more or less and*

misserable marches we have had for deep and miry roads and through tedious woods and wildernesses and over vast high rocks and mountaines, that it may be easily judged what our little army endured and what unusuall hardship they went through.

The French armies had been pulled away from the vulnerable Dutch border, but Marlborough's army was in its turn exposed while on the move. If Bedmar in the Moselle valley, or Tallard in Alsace, had just once spotted Marlborough's plan soon enough, they could quickly move to fall on the flank of the marching columns and trains. With Villeroi's army closing up behind, Marlborough would face two enemy forces, and disaster might result, with his troops a long way from their bases, out of position and outnumbered. Such a danger depended upon the French realising the Duke's intentions. This they failed to do – the march to the Danube was too daring a project, too imaginative for French Marshals who, in their turn, were too accustomed to turning to their king in Versailles for advice on operational matters. Puzzled, they watched Marlborough march past and away from their grasp. Eventually, Tallard and Villeroi met in Alsace and appealed to Louis XIV for instructions: 'You, who understand the ways of war so much better than we.' The King sent an order that Tallard should take his corps to reinforce Marshal Marsin, who was already in Bavaria. Villeroi was to remain and hold the Alsace frontier secure, and prevent those Imperial German and Dutch troops on the Rhine from going with Marlborough over the Swabian Jura hills to the Danube valley.

After passing Heidelberg, Marlborough's army turned eastwards at Wiesloch, heading through pleasant farmland towards Württemberg. The Neckar was crossed near to Heilbronn and, on 10 June 1704, at the small village of Mundleheim, Marlborough met for the first time the President of the Imperial War Council, Prince Eugene of Savoy, who came to the Duke's camp with Count Wratislaw. The two commanders immediately struck up a close and valuable friendship. The next day Eugene inspected and complimented the quality of Marlborough's cavalry and dragoons, and two days later, on 13 June, the Imperial Field Commander, the Margrave of Baden, joined them at the Inn of the Golden Fleece in Gross Heppach. Baden, however, was not an easy colleague to deal with. He was proud and obstinate, and had learned his trade as a soldier in a

Allied grenadier (left) and 'hatman', c.1704. By kind permission of His Grace the Duke of Marlborough.

more sedate school than Marlborough. He was brave enough, as events would prove, but given the choice would march and counter-march to try and catch an enemy at a disadvantage, then sit down to besiege towns rather than engage in brutal battle on an open field. This manner of war was less risky to reputations and, perhaps, less expensive in highly trained troops than Marlborough's way, and so the two men could not easily agree how to proceed. However, Eugene had built a formidable reputation as a fighter against the Turks, and his way of war was much more akin to that of Marlborough. The Prince also had his doubts regarding Baden's reliability, for he was a close friend of the renegade Elector of Bavaria – they had shared many a campaign against the Turks together in past years. It was suspected that Baden was even now corresponding with his old comrade in an indiscreet way.

The plan for the coming campaign that the Margrave now outlined to his two colleagues was quite sound, as far as it went. He and Marlborough would operate independently in an encirclement of the Elector's army. This would both offer the prospect of overwhelming the French and Bavarian forces before reinforcements arrived from the Rhine, and permit each commander to exercise authority over his own troops, unhampered by the presence of the other. It had already been agreed that Eugene would go to command the Imperial and Dutch troops on the Upper Rhine at the Lines of Stollhofen, and to prevent support being sent to Marsin and the Elector from the French armies there. However, the first part of this plan could not proceed, as the Danish contingent under the Duke of Württemburg was making slow time in marching to join the Allied army. Until they came Marlborough did not have enough strength to operate in Bavaria independently. However, as an indication of the high trust that reposed in Marlborough at the political level at this time, he received full authority from London and the Hague to make a treaty with the Elector of Bavaria, on such terms as he saw fit, if the opportunity arose.

On 14 June Eugene left for the Rhine, and Marlborough made the best of having to work with Baden. He wrote to a friend in London from his camp at Ebersbach:

Prince Eugene went post for the Rhine, where he was to arrive this morning [15 June]*, and Prince Louis* [Baden] *is to be at the same time with his army on the Danube. I followed* *our troops hither, intending to join him in a few days, it being agreed that we act in conjunction for ten or twelve days till the next of the troops come up. We propose to march directly to the Elector, who, it is thought, will either retire over the Danube or march to his strong camp at Dillingen and Lavingen.*

To complicate things the Dutch once again pleaded for the return of their troops, but Marlborough turned a deaf ear to them. He wrote to his close friend Hiensius, the Grand Pensionary of Holland:

I beg you will take care that I receive no orders from the States [General] *that may put me out of a condition of reducing the Elector, for that would be of all mischiefs the greatest.*

One obstacle to be crossed before the campaign could progress was the steep Geislingen pass in the Jura hills. The weather continued to be bad and the roads were in dreadful condition. The marching pace of the soldiers slowed accordingly, and Marlborough's army would be vulnerable to attack as it threaded its way through the pass. The Elector of Bavaria might move to block the route, and if the rearguard and baggage train of the Allied army were threatened by the French, the main body could hardly turn about to support them.

The Elector of Bavaria chose not to take the initiative, and news was received in the Allied camp that his army had fallen back: 'We have advice that the Elector has re-passed the Danube with all his troops' the Duke wrote to London. A message came from the Margrave of Baden that his Imperial troops had secured the head of the pass, and so Marlborough's army plunged in, and came through safely. On 22 June 1704 the marching troops met those of the Margrave at Launsheim on the northern approaches to Bavaria. Their combined forces comprised 60,000 men and the Duke now had a distinct superiority in numbers against any of the French columns ponderously manoeuvring against him.

With the Allied armies now combined, the Elector and Marshal Marsin, conscious of their weakness in numbers before French reinforcements arrived, put their 40,000-strong army into an entrenched camp at Dillingen on the north bank of the Danube. Marlborough had been unable to bring siege guns from the Low Countries and Baden failed to supply any (despite assurances that he would do so). So, the Duke could not attack the Elector in his camp, and had to manoeuvre to cross the Danube at another

The Wings of an Army

In the early 18th century it was common practice for armies in the field to comprise two Wings, which functioned in a similar manner to a modern army corps (except that, unlike the present-day formations, they were not self-sufficient and would rarely operate independently). Each Wing would be commanded by a general officer of broadly equal rank who, in turn, would report to the army commander.

At Blenheim however, the Allied army had Prince Eugene's Wing on the right and the Duke of Marlborough's Wing on the left. Eugene deferred to Marlborough as commanding general in the planning and execution of the battle. He followed the Duke's orders and threw his smaller Wing into an expensive attack to fix his opponent and prevent co-operation between the different parts of their opponents' armies. This worked well, despite the strains of that long summer afternoon, because of the trust and friendship existing between the two men. The French and Bavarian armies at Blenheim operated differently. The Elector of Bavaria, by virtue of his rank, was the more senior commander there, but his own depleted army was just a fraction of the size of the French forces present. The two Marshals, Tallard and Marsin, paid lip-service to deferring to the Elector, but there was little co-operation or contact between them. Partly this had to do with the fear of glanders infection (a highly infectious disease affecting horses) from Tallard's cavalry on the right. Marsin refused to move to Tallard's support later in the day and the two Wings of the French and Bavarians fought their own battle almost entirely separately, as if they were two distinct armies, neither of which had a stake in the success of the other.

Care must be taken when reading accounts of the battles at this time not to confuse the movements of the two Wings. The right Wing might be holding the left flank, while the left Wing prepared to attack on the right.

The 18th century stone bridge over the River Wörnitz at Ebermorgen. Marlborough's troops crossed here to attack the Schellenberg.

point, hoping to force the French and Bavarians out into the open where they could be brought to battle. The lines of supply and communication for the Duke's army were now established into Franconia and central Germany. These were fairly secure from raids, but his present supply base, at Nordlingen, was too far to the north to be convenient, once the line of the Danube was crossed. So, the Duke had to look around for an alternative, and his eye fell on Donauwörth. The small pretty town offered a good river crossing, and a secure forward base, but it was overlooked by the 'Hill of the Bell', the Schellenberg.

The village of Blindheim from the west, as it appears today.

Chapter 3

BREAKING INTO BAVARIA

AS MARLBOROUGH'S ARMY neared Donauwörth on the Danube he received interesting information regarding the measures that the Elector of Bavaria was taking to repulse him. Marlborough's chaplain, Dr Francis Hare, wrote:

> Some 13,000 of the enemy were encamped upon the Schellenberg and they were very busy in fortifying and entrenching themselves. His Grace sent out the Quartermaster-General [Cadogan] with a party of 400 horse to gain more particular intelligence.

In fact, Count Jean D'Arco, a Piedmontese officer in Bavarian service, had been sent from the camp at Dillingen with about 12,000 men to hold the grassy hill and the walled town. He had sixteen Bavarian and seven French infantry battalions, six squadrons of French and three squadrons of Bavarian dragoons, and sixteen guns. This was a potent force and the troops were of good quality, led by veteran officers. In addition, Donauwörth town was held by a regular French infantry battalion and two battalions of Bavarian militia. However, the nearly seventy-year-old defences on the hill, built by the Swedish king, Gustavus Adolphus, during the Thirty Years War, were neglected and broken down. The walls of the town were second rate and had little of Vauban's sophistication to ward off assault. Getting his men into place on 30 June 1704, D'Arco set them to improve the breastwork across the Schellenberg, and conscripted local peasants to help with the labouring task. Several of the locals who fled to avoid impressment came to the Allied camp with news of the preparations on the hill.

Private John Deane would be among those who went into action on the Schellenberg:

> The enemy was incampt upon the hill called Schellinburgh neare to the toune of Danuwert, being the strongest pass in all Germany and they had made it stronger than ordinary this yeare by reason they heard of the English army coming to make them a visitte.

The Margrave of Baden protested when he learned that

29

Op't Donauwaerd, naer by den Schellenberg gelegen,
lang de waerelt, staet vol pralen met den Zegen
Bestaelt door Marlborough door Baden, Beyerschen Graf
En met te wekeren Boom vlugt d'Keere waereld d'sin

Marlborough had plans for an outright assault, arguing, with good reason, that casualties were sure to be severe. However, despite the obvious need for co-operation, Marlborough had the most authority, as the representative of Queen Anne, by now the paymaster of the Imperial armies. The Duke was aware that every day that passed allowed the Elector to strengthen the defences on the hill, as the movement of the Allied army towards the river crossings at Donauwörth could not be entirely hidden. Accordingly, on 30 June the Allied army was marching eastwards to Amerdingen, fifteen miles short of Donauwörth. Matters became urgent on 1 July, when a messenger came in from Prince Eugene with news that Tallard had eluded him and was even now marching with another French army through the Black Forest to reinforce Marshal Marsin and the Elector. If Marlborough did not force the line of the Danube quickly, and carry the war into the Elector's lands now, he might never do so.

The Schellenberg was to be subject to a direct storm, as time did not allow Marlborough to manoeuvre D'Arco out of position. The Duke selected 130 men from each of the battalions of the Allied army, a body of 5,850 troops in total. These were the grenadiers and other volunteers for the dangerous task as stormers. A forlorn hope of eighty men was drawn from the 1st English Foot Guards, commanded by Lord John Mordaunt and Colonel Richard Munden, who would spearhead the attack. Marlborough could not spare the time for the main body of the Allied army to close up. Accordingly, he formed a second echelon for the attack, which comprised two 'divisions', each of eight battalions (British, Dutch, Hanoverian and Hessian), under command of Withers and Horn. Backing them would be thirty-five squadrons of British and Dutch cavalry and dragoons, led by Henry Lumley and Graf Reynard van Hompesch. Lastly, Baden, whose Wing of the army was behind that of Marlborough on the march, would hold a brigade of Imperial grenadiers ready for action whenever the opportunity came, as there was not sufficient room in front of the Schellenberg for them to fully deploy. Colonel Holcroft Blood would bring a battery of guns into action near the hamlet of Berg, just to the north of Donauwörth, to support the attack, and the Margrave would also provide a battery for this task. In all, Marlborough was deploying about 22,000 men in this bold and brutally direct operation.

31

Graf Reynard Vincent van Hompesch (1660–1733). Commanded Dutch cavalry at the Schellenberg and Blenheim.

In the early hours of 2 July 1704, the Allied army began their march to battle. The roads were muddy and progress slower than expected, but the fast-flowing Wörnitz river at Ebermorgen was crossed by mid-afternoon. Their approach had been seen during the morning by D'Arco's outposts, and Marlborough, who was spotted carrying out his own close reconnaissance of the defensive preparations on the Schellenberg, was fired on briefly. However, the Duke had time to see that the ground beyond the Danube was also being prepared for a camp. Tent lines were being marked out, ready for the arrival of substantial numbers of troops, and it was evident that D'Arco expected to be reinforced, probably on the following day. As if in response, the Duke ordered his Quartermaster-General, William Cadogan, to begin to mark out a camp well short of the Wörnitz, to give the impression that the army would spend the night there, rather than mounting an attack immediately. Time seemed to be on the side of the defenders as the afternoon wore on. D'Arco, who expected to be joined by the Elector of Bavaria and his main force the following day, was quite relaxed at news of the Allied approach, and leaving the supervision of the still incomplete defences on the hill, he went to have lunch with the French commander of Donauwörth, Colonel DuBordet.

Meanwhile, as the marching columns poured across the Wörnitz and approached the dark hill, the Bavarian outposts set fire to the hamlet of Berg, and hurried off to give the alarm. D'Arco, rudely interrupted from his comfortable lunch, took horse and galloped up the slope of the hill, calling his labouring soldiers to drop shovels and take up their arms. Colonel Jean De La Colonie, a French officer who fought that day in the Bavarian service, wrote afterwards:

> *The Schellenberg height is oval in plan, with a gentle slope on the southern side, which affords very easy communication with Donauwert; whilst on the northern [side] the country is covered with very thick woods and undergrowth reaching close up to the old entrenchments.*

These thick woods and undergrowth (known then as the Boschberg) limited Marlborough's freedom of action; he had to throw his stormers into the battle on a very narrow front. Among the marching Allied soldiers nearing the hill was a female dragoon, Christian Welsh (subsequently known as Mrs Davies or Mother Ross), and she remembered:

33

Our vanguard did not come into sight on the enemy entrenchments til the afternoon; however, not to give the Bavarians time to make themselves yet stronger, the duke ordered the Dutch General Goor who commanded the right Wing, comprised of English and Dutch with some auxiliary troops, to attack, as soon as possible.

The attack went in just after 6pm, the soldiers tramping across the boggy Kaiback stream to get to the foot of the hill. Blood's gunners pounded the defenders from a battery position near to Berg, and caused havoc among the French infantry, exposed on the higher slope above the breastwork which was manned by the Bavarians. De La Colonie wrote that he was drenched in the blood and brains of one of his officers, the Comte de la Bastide, with almost the first shot: 'The enemy's battery opened fire on us, and raked us through and through.' The Allied stormers had each been handed a bundle of fascines (sticks) with which to bridge any ditch obstacles. The soldiers wastefully threw these away into a dry gully as they toiled up the slope, which was heavy going despite De La Colonie's casual assertion that the gradient was gentle. The French and Bavarians watched their approach in silence, the only sound being the tapping of a French drummer trying to hide the intimidating shouts and hurrahs of the advancing enemy. As the range closed the panting Allied soldiers were suddenly swept by heavy volleys of musketry and canister from the breastworks and the battery above them. John Deane described the opening phase of the assault:

No sooner did our Forlorne Hope appear but the enemy did throw in their volleys of canon balls and small shott among them and made a brave defence an a bold resistance against us as brave loyall hearted gentlemen souldiers ought to for there prince and country.

Scores of the leading attackers were tumbled down in the blast, and the confusion was made worse by handfuls of fizzing hand grenades, which were showered easily down the slope into the toiling ranks. With superb discipline though, the gaps were closed up and the attackers pressed forward towards the defences, where a savage contest with bayonet and musket butt began, wherever the soldiers could reach each other. The ditch running across the front of the breastwork caused terrible difficulty, as the attackers now had no fascines. Johan Wigand van Goor, the Dutch general officer leading the assault, was killed, and many of the regimental officers, conspicuous in the laced coats, were shot down. Colonel Munden, leading the forlorn hope of English Guards, remembered that his hat was all shot to pieces by musket balls, but he came through the day unhurt.

With broken ranks and in confusion, the stormers fell back down the slopes, away from the tormenting fire of the defenders. Exultantly, scores of Bavarian grenadiers came pouring over their breastwork to drive their opponents to defeat at the foot of the hill. They were too rash, for the second echelon of Allied infantry, under Henry Withers, were just moving into position to support the attack. Orkney's Regiment and the 1st English Foot Guards met the counter-attack with solid volleys and the slopes were now strewn with Bavarian dead and wounded too. The grenadiers scrambled back into cover as Marlborough's renewed attack went in and, once again, the fire of the defenders

William, 1st Earl Cadogan (1665–1726). Marlborough's Quartermaster-General.

broke up the Allied ranks. Count von Styrum dismounted and went forward on foot to encourage the soldiers, but he too was promptly killed and the attackers fell back once again to recover their order. The ground in front of the breastworks was grotesquely choked with the wreckage of their attack.

Marlborough now ordered his squadrons of cavalry and dragoons to close up to the foot of the hill, along the line of the Kaiback stream. As Dr Hare put it 'the Horse and Dragoons stood so close and animated the Foot so much that they rallied and went in again.' This move, of course, made it difficult for any waverers among the assault squads to make off to a place of greater safety, but Marlborough's chaplain was too delicate to say so. Thus encouraged, the Allied attack was pressed forward through a vicious volume of musketry the like of which, it was afterwards said, had never before been seen on a battlefield. Despite the gallantry of the Allied soldiers, many of whom now had no officers to command them, the defence was as sturdy as ever, casualties were appalling, and a dangerous stalemate seemed to have been reached.

At this crucial point, Marlborough learned from a soldier, who had drifted off to the right of the attack, that a line of wicker basket gabions, linking the town walls with the breastwork on the hill, was quite unoccupied. The French troops stationed there by D'Arco, the Nectancourt Régiment, had been drawn into the desperate fighting on the hill, and the left flank of his position was laid bare. An officer went spurring to find Baden, but the Margrave had already seen the chance and was hurrying his grenadiers forward from Berg towards the Kaiback. Little troubled by scattered shots from the walls of the town, the Imperial troops were able to form up at the foot of the Schellenberg, staring upwards at the raw open flank of D'Arco's position.

Despite other pressing demands on his attention, the approach of Baden's men along the small stream had not gone unnoticed by Count D'Arco, and he hurried to the rear to summon forward the dismounted French dragoons, held back in the lee of the hill. This was a mistake: the dragoons attempted to advance against the flank of the Imperial soldiers as they climbed the hill, but were thrown back by the volleys of three companies of grenadiers who turned half-right to face them. The shaken dragoons were reluctant to try again, and D'Arco found himself out of position and out of contact with the main body of his troops fighting for their lives on the crest of the hill.

At the breastwork the deadly struggle continued, and Count Maffei, now the senior Bavarian commander in the defences, saw the grey-coated Imperial grenadiers steadily approaching from the direction of the town. In the dust and the smoke of the battle recognition was tricky and some officers called out to those around them not to fire, as they must surely be reinforcements from DuBordet's garrison in Donauwörth. Almost immediately they realised the error, as Baden's troops began to form their line of battle actually in the rear of the French and Bavarian position. Their musketry volleys swept through the ranks of the defenders, many of whom, taken completely by surprise, were suddenly called on by their officers to change front and face to the left to meet the new and wholly unexpected threat. Confusion resulted,

Imperial Austrian grenadier and infantrymen, c.1704.

as Marlborough's stormers scrambled over the suddenly weakly held breastwork and, supported by a fresh echelon of dismounted British dragoons sent in by the Duke, pressed resolutely onward, crowding the defenders back towards the crown of the hill. Colonel De La Colonie wrote that:

> They [Baden's grenadiers] *arrived within gunshot of our flank about 7.30 in the evening, without our being aware of the possibility of such a thing, so occupied were we in the defence of our own particular post and the confidence we had as to the safety of the rest of our position.*

The turning of their flank was fatal and the infection of panic set in:

> *My men had no sooner got clear of the entrenchments than they found that the slope was in their favour, and they fairly broke and took to flight, in order to reach the plain that lay before them before the enemy's cavalry could get upon their track. I found myself entirely alone on the height, prevented from running by my heavy boots.*

The French and Bavarian defenders, after a gallant defence but hopelessly out-numbered and out-manoeuvred, were running for

French grenadier, c.1704.

safety. Marlborough had anticipated the collapse and his squadrons of cavalry were well closed up. These were now sent in ruthless pursuit of the broken defenders, who were chased, harried and chopped down without mercy. The dragoons also remounted to take their part in the bloody work. Count D'Arco, with his army in broken flight beyond hope of recovery, hurried to the sanctuary of the walls of Donauwörth, as did Maffei, but it took prolonged hammering on the gates to induce the nervous garrison to admit the fugitive commanders. The Bavarian gunners on the hill, professional to the last, sacrificed themselves to spike their guns before the Allies got their hands on them.

While light lasted the pursuit was pressed and many of D'Arco's soldiers, attempting to cross the Danube, were drowned in the murky waters. A pontoon bridge erected there collapsed under the weight of fugitives, and rain added to the misery of the fugitives, and the masses of wounded men of both armies who littered the hill. Mrs Davies wrote that

> 'We made a cruel slaughter of them and the bridge over the Danube breaking down, a great number were drowned.'

All the guns on the Schellenberg were captured by the Allies, as were the regimental colours of all the French and Bavarian battalions but one; the exception was De La Colonie's Grenadiers Rouge Régiment who, despite the speed of their flight, managed to keep together, more or less. The immensely valuable Bavarian engineer pontoon train was left at the riverbank for Marlborough to seize.

So devastating was the defeat that, of the 12,000 troops deployed in defence of the Schellenberg, no more than about 3,000 men ever rallied to the colours. The numbers of Bavarians and French killed that day are not known, but over 2,000 unwounded prisoners were taken by the Allies. These soldiers were the best the Elector of Bavaria had, and the destruction of D'Arco's corps in this way had a profound effect on the ability of Marlborough's opponents to face him in the coming campaign.

Such victories are not to be had easily, and Marlborough's army paid a severe price for its triumph. Of the 22,000 troops engaged in the assault, some 1,400 were killed and over 4,000 wounded (1,500 of the casualties were British, every third man in the line that day). Only seventeen of Mordaunt's forlorn hope survived the day. The hospitals that the Duke had set up in Nordlingen were overwhelmed with the numbers of the wounded, and the 'widows' of the army were instructed to report there to tend the stricken soldiers (at least one of whom was also a woman). Among the fallen were seven general officers, including the Margrave of Baden who was shot in the foot. Fine officers such as Goor and von Stryum had died and would be sadly missed by Marlborough. Still, Donauwörth was abandoned by Colonel DuBordet that night and the Duke had a forward base for the coming operations, and the vital crossing point over the

Emperor Leopold I of Austria. Died 1705 and was succeeded by his son, Joseph I.

Danube was firmly in his hands. Congratulations on the daring success came to his camp from many quarters, although some voiced consternation at the scale of the losses. Perhaps the most expressive tribute was that from the Emperor Leopold, whose capital of Vienna was suddenly no longer under such threat. The victory, he wrote to Marlborough in his own hand (an unusual honour), was due to 'the wonderful ardour and constancy of the forces under your command.'

Getting across the Danube was one thing, but forcing peace on the Elector of Bavaria was quite another. Shocked at the destruction of D'Arco's corps, which he had viewed in person from the far side of the river, the Elector knew that his position at Dillingen was no longer tenable. He abandoned the line of the Danube, drew his garrisons out of Nieuberg and Ratisbon, and fell back southwards, coming to rest behind the shelter of the River Lech, taking up a position near to Augsburg. Although, in his alarm at the defeat, the Elector sent envoys to Marlborough to discuss peace terms, it turned out that he was just playing for time, hoping to blunt the Allied campaign while Marshal Tallard and his French army drew nearer. The Electress, more pragmatic than her volatile husband, begged him to negotiate seriously with Marlborough, but the Elector put his faith in the French.

Although reinforcements were daily joining the Allied army – the Danish cavalry arrived on 6 July 1704 – time was not on Marlborough's side. The town of Nieuburg had been abandoned by the Bavarians, which further freed Marlborough's lines of communication and supply northwards. His advanced detachments crossed the Lech river on pontoon bridges at Gunderkingen on 9 July, feeling out the strength of opposition. However, the lack of a proper siege train hampered operations and the reduction of Rain was a tedious and time-consuming operation. The Duke wrote to London on 13 July:

> *We have been waiting the arrival of the great guns from Nuremberg, in order to attack Rain, where there is a garrison of about a thousand men, which is not thought advisable to leave behind us. Nine twenty-four pounders came up yesterday and we are hourly expecting three more, so that this night we shall break ground and hope to have our batteries fixed tomorrow.*

Later the same day Marlborough wrote to another acquaintance:

> *You will have seen that our success on the Schellenberg has been followed by the passage of the Danube and the Lech without any opposition, and the enemy's quitting of Nieuberg; but we have met with a disappointment in the want of our artillery from Nuremberg for attacking Rain.*

The small town of Rain on the Lech river fell to Marlborough on 16 July. He then marched his army towards Munich and sowed alarm throughout Bavaria, but then turned aside to face the Elector and Marsin at Augsburg. On 18 July the Allied army closed up to the Lech at Friedburg. The Duke had won the strategic prize of placing his numerically stronger army between the French and Bavarians and the city of Vienna. All the same, so exasperated was he at the prevarication of the Elector, that on 26 July Marlborough, having swept clean of provisions the countryside along the Lech, let loose his cavalry and dragoons on a campaign of fire and sword across the rich lands south of the Danube. This had two aims: firstly, to put pressure on the Elector to make peace; and, secondly, to ruin Bavaria as a base from which the French and Bavarian armies could either attack Vienna or pursue the Duke into Franconia if he had to withdraw northwards. Autumn was approaching and if he could not force a decision on the Danube before winter Marlborough must withdraw his army into central Germany to provision itself and find billets. The Dutch would almost certainly demand the return of their own troops, and the Duke's whole plan would be in ruins.

For miles Bavarian hamlets and villages were put to the torch, after cattle and crops were seized for the commissaries of the Allied army. 'With fire and sword the country round was wasted far and wide, and many a nursing mother then and suckling baby died.' Baden protested to Marlborough at the supposed barbarity of the campaign, so the Duke ordered him to use his own Imperial cavalry on the stern operations rather than the British, German,

Mrs Christian Davies

Illustration of Mrs Christian Davies (also known as Christopher Welsh/Walsh and Mother Ross)

Born in Dublin in 1667, this redoubtable female concealed her identity and enlisted in the army as a man in 1693 in Captain Tichborne's Company, in order to follow her soldier husband to the wars. She was at the battle of Landen (1693) and was captured by the French soon afterwards, but her deception remained undetected. Having transferred to Teviot's Dragoons in 1695, she fought at Namur, and returned to Ireland on release from the service after the Treaty of Ryswick (1697).

In 1701 Christian Welsh enlisted again and went with Marlborough's army to the Danube in the summer of 1704. Wounded in the thigh at the Schellenberg fight, she recovered sufficiently to take part in the Battle of Blenheim 'wherein I took no hurt.' However, returning to Holland, Welsh found her errant husband at last, although he was dallying with a Dutch woman. It seems that she had acquired a strong taste for the soldier's life, and her man kept the secret safe.

At Ramillies (1706) Welsh was shot and wounded again, and was too stunned to conceal her sex. She was dismissed from the regiment (now Hay's Dragoons), but, because of her good character as a soldier, was permitted to remain with the army, as a sutleress. Richard Welsh was killed at Malplaquet (1709) and Christian wrote movingly of her vain search for him in the front line during that dreadful battle. She recovered her spirits enough to marry again a few weeks later, wedding Hugh Jones, a grenadier in the Royal Scots, but he was killed at the siege of St Venant in 1710.

After the Treaty of Utrecht (1713) Christian Jones went to England and kept a public house. Her third husband, an ex-soldier named Davies, drank the profits and she faced destitution, until she was admitted to the Royal Hospital at Chelsea as an in-pensioner. Mrs Christian Davies recounted her intriguing career to Daniel Defoe before her death in July 1739, when she was buried with full military honours at St Margaret's, Westminster.

Danish and Dutch. However, the Duke was sensitive to the adverse comments, and wrote to his wife to say that the English cavalry had no part in the devastation. That was irrelevant (and not true) as it was Marlborough who gave the order, no matter which troops were involved. The responsibility was his and the soldiers thought none the less of him for it. Mrs Christian Davies, still serving with Hay's Dragoons (Royal Scots Greys) despite wounds received in the recent battle, wrote of the conduct of the Allied soldiery in the Danube campaign:

The allies sent parties on every hand to ravage the country, who pillaged above fifty villages, burnt the houses of peasants and gentlemen, and forced the inhabitants, with what few cattle had escaped the insatiable enemy, to seek refuge in the woods. We miserably plundered the poor inhabitants of this electorate. I had left the hospital time enough to contribute to their misery and to have a share in the plunder. We spared nothing, killing, burning or otherwise destroying whatever we could not carry off.

This burning of Bavaria was a ruthless act of war, but some observers felt the scale of the devastation was exaggerated, perhaps for propaganda purposes. Colonel De La Colonie wrote:

I followed a route through several villages said to have been reduced to cinders, and although I certainly found a few burnt houses, still the damage was as nothing compared with the reports current through the country.

However, Samuel Noyes, one of Marlborough's officers, wrote that: 'In this last march particularly we entirely burnt a mighty pretty village with a noble church and cloister'. In any case, the destruction, on whatever scale, was justified militarily, for the Elector was obliged to disperse much of his small army to protect his estates. With no richly stocked countryside left to supply the voracious demands of the French and Bavarian armies, the Elector's ability to campaign was, at best, foundering, and he must now trust that time would run out for his opponent.

All this while the French army under Marshal Tallard was struggling through the tangled passes of the Black Forest. It had eluded Prince Eugene's vigilance on the Rhine, but the predatory foraging customs by which the French troops fed themselves earned the hatred of the peasantry of the unfortunate regions through which they marched. Their advanced guards fought a continual battle to clear the roads of partisans and desperate

Ferdinand, Comte de Marsin,
Marshal of France (1656–1706).

villagers, while brigands closed around their rearguard to murder couriers, harry foragers and pick off stragglers. To add to their troubles, the French cavalry found their horses falling prey to glanders (known at the time as the 'German Sickness') and they were not in top condition on arrival in Bavaria as a result. The veteran Swiss troops in French service had exercised their right under the terms of their enlistment not to campaign beyond the Rhine frontier, and Louis XIV decided that they should not be coerced. Accordingly, numbers of inexperienced French infantry battalions were sent to replace them, and marched with Tallard to Bavaria.

After wasting several days by laying siege to Villingen, Tallard drew off on learning of Eugene's approach. The Prince had brought only 20,000 men, as the Lines of Stollhofen could not be left unguarded. Making as good time as his enormous supply train allowed, the Marshal delivered the wagons to the depots in Ulm and then combined his 34,000-strong army with that of Marsin and the Elector on 6 August 1704, at Biberbach. Tallard was not impressed to find that, as he had suspected, not only were the depots and magazines in Bavaria inadequate to provision his army for very long without further re-supply from beyond the Rhine, but the Elector had also dispersed his army in response to Marlborough's campaign of ravaging the region. He wrote to French War Minister Chamillart later of the Elector's attitude at this critical time:

> *There was the total ignorance of the enemy's strength, and M de Baviere* [the Elector] *having all his troops, except five battalions and about twenty-seven squadrons, spread out about the country to cover his salt-works, a gentleman's private estate in fact, instead of what they should have guarded – his frontiers.*

Marsin was just as scathing in his own reports, concerning the

The respective strengths of the armies at Blenheim

ALLIED ARMY

Left Wing (Marlborough)

British	14 Battalions	14 Squadrons
Dutch	12 Battalions	20 Squadrons
Hessians	7 Battalions	7 Squadrons
Hanoverians	11 Battalions	20 Squadrons
Danes		4 Squadrons
40 Guns		

Total **32,000** men

Right Wing (Eugene)

Austrians		29 Squadrons
Imperial Germans		35 Squadrons
Prussians	11 Battalions	15 Squadrons
Danes	7 Battalions	
20 Guns		

Total **20,000** men

FRENCH AND BAVARIAN ARMY

Left Wing (Marsin and the Elector of Bavaria)

Bavarians	5 Battalions	27 Squadrons
French	33 Battalions	40 Squadrons
45 Guns		

Total **30,000** men

Right Wing (Tallard)

French	36 Battalions	64 Squadrons
45 Guns		12 Squadrons
		of dismounted
Total **26,000** men		dragoons

lack of co-operation in the campaign by the Elector:

The Elector has 35 good battalions and 43 squadrons of good troops, of which since the entry of the enemy into Bavaria he has had [only] *23 squadrons and 5 battalions with the army.*

Eugene had hovered around Tallard's flank during the passage through the Black Forest, but with his lack of numbers could not seriously disrupt the march. The same day that the French and

Bavarian armies met near Augsburg, the Prince encamped his small army on the plain of Höchstädt on the north bank of the Danube. That evening of 6 August he rode to confer with Marlborough at Schrobenhausen just south of Donauwörth, accompanied by only a single trooper as escort. In an intriguing twist to the campaign, the Margrave had suggested that he should take his own Imperial troops to besiege the Bavarian-held fortress of Ingolstadt on the Danube some miles below Donauwörth. This was a plan discussed earlier in the campaign, but shelved at the time. Now, happy to have the obstinate, and possibly unreliable, Imperial general out of the way, Marlborough agreed to this operation with alacrity. After conferring with his colleagues over the following two days, Baden marched off eastwards with a corps of over 12,000 infantry and 3,700 cavalry on the evening of 9 August.

The Duke allowed Baden to go, and gave up a precious numerical advantage in the process. Now, 56,000 French and Bavarian troops were facing 52,000 British, Dutch, Danish, German and Imperial soldiers. The Duke plainly felt the price worth the paying. He and Eugene were about to embark on a campaign of the most daring and dangerous kind, and it had little hope of success while the obstinate Margrave was on the scene.

The junction of the armies, August 1704.

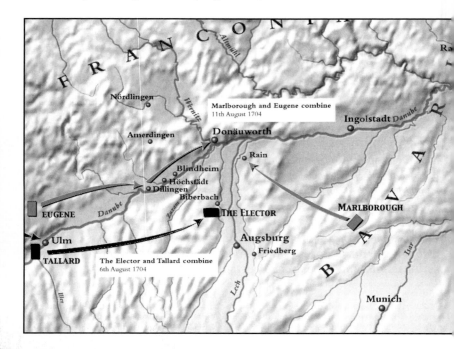

Chapter 4

FORCING THE NARROW WAY

HE TWO FRENCH MARSHALS, Tallard and Marsin, and the Elector of Bavaria had combined their armies near Augsburg, and they now felt confident enough to challenge their opponents, while the two Wings of the Allied army were apart – Marlborough at Rain to the south of the Danube and Eugene about twenty miles away at Höchstädt on the north bank. If either could be caught while in this way separated, the French and Bavarians should be able to overwhelm their less numerous opponent, and the whole Allied campaign on the Danube would be over. Eugene, with the smaller force, seemed the more vulnerable, but Marlborough could not move quickly to combine with him until he was sure that their opponents had crossed to the north bank of the Danube. To do so prematurely might risk the Margrave of Baden at Ingolstadt becoming prey to a French and Bavarian raid, if nothing worse, mounted south of the river.

It seemed that Tallard would have preferred to bide his time, replenish his supplies, and allow Marlborough's Danube campaign to wither away in the colder weeks of autumn. The region was unfamiliar to the Marshal, and there was some doubt about the strength of the Allied army. To wait seemed the prudent course and, meanwhile, further reinforcements and supplies would be summoned from the Rhine – the remaining Imperial troops at the Lines of Stollhofen had not the strength to prevent them. However, Marsin was an ambitious man, newly created a Marshal of France, and he had a reputation to make. The Elector too was anxious to push the pace of their campaign, for it was on his lands that the

Tapfheim Church. Marlborough and Eugene viewed Tallard's camp from the tower on 12 August 1704.

Allied armies were exercising their talent for barn-burning. He was not a ruler particularly sensitive to the needs of his people, but he could not ignore their plight for ever: revolution might result, and before long his own estates might become the target for destruction. Tallard and the Elector had some sharp conversations over whether to wait or to advance. The veteran Marshal, replying to the Bavarian's scoffing at his caution, said: 'I should imagine that you wished to gamble with the King's forces, without having any of your own, to see at no risk what would happen.' The allusion to the continued dispersal of the Elector's own army on guard duties is clear. Tallard added the obvious truth, in a letter to Versailles, that it was 'a sound lesson never to have more than one man in command of an army' and what a misfortune it was to have to control a prince like the Elector of Bavaria. Anyway, the French and Bavarian commanders at last decided to strike at Eugene. On 9 August, as Baden marched eastwards to Ingolstadt, their armies began crossing the Danube on pontoon bridges to the now derelict camp at Dillingen, a few miles to the west of Höchstädt. Eugene was in a very exposed position, and he wrote to the Duke on 10 August 1704:

> The enemy have marched. It is almost certain that the whole army is passing the Danube at Lauingen. They have pushed a Lieutenant-Colonel who I sent to reconnoitre back to Hochstadt. The Plain of Dillingen is crowded with troops. I have held on all day here; but with 18 battalions I dare not risk staying the night. I quit [the position] however with much regret being good and if he [Tallard] takes it, it will cost us much to get it back. Everything, milord, consists in speed and that you put yourself forthwith in movement to join me tomorrow. While I was writing sure news has reached me that the whole army has crossed.

The Prince prudently drew his troops eastwards along the course of the Danube towards Donauwörth, and sent pioneers ahead to prepare fresh defences on the Schellenberg in case of need. In moving away he subtly but certainly pulled the French and Bavarians forward from their river crossing places and into position to be the target for a sudden attack.

Marlborough learned on the evening of 10 August, from his own scouts, that the French and Bavarians had crossed to the north bank of the Danube. He at once detached twenty-seven squadrons of cavalry, under the Prince of Württemberg, to support Eugene, and a strong detachment of twenty battalions of infantry under his younger brother, Charles Churchill, followed. The following day the Duke wrote:

> *We thought it advisable that he* [Eugene] *should be reinforced, and that the whole army should advance nearer the Danube in order to join him if the enemy passed [the river]; upon which I ordered the Duke-Regent of Wirtemberg to march early this morning to reinforce the prince.*

Maximilien - Emmanuel Wittelsbach, Elector of Bavaria (1796-1736).

Marlborough and Eugene met that night at Münster, to the west of Donauwörth, and the junction of their armies was safely achieved in the afternoon of 11 August 1704 on the Kessel stream.

News that Baden had been detached to Ingolstadt was rumoured in the Elector's camp that very evening. If this proved to be so, the Allied army, even when combined, was quite correctly thought to be fewer in numbers and guns than that which their opponents could deploy on the plain of Höchstädt. It seemed to the French and Bavarian commanders that Marlborough had fumbled his campaign. He had not prevented them from combining their own armies, and had then allowed Baden to go off with a powerful corps on what was plainly a secondary operation. So it appeared that the initiative in the campaign now lay firmly with the stronger army. This was a comforting thought, but the French and Bavarians were becoming careless and in the presence of such opponents as Marlborough and Eugene the price for carelessness would be heavy.

During 11 August Tallard and his colleagues pushed forward from the river crossings at Dillingen, past the marshy ground along the Pulver and Brunnen streams near Höchstädt, to encamp their 56,000 men and 90 guns amid the comparatively dry and lush cornfields between the villages of Lutzingen, Oberglau and Blindheim. In doing so they over-ran some small forward detachments of Eugene's troops. The site they occupied enjoyed the open, level plain stretching for four miles from the banks of the Danube river to the wooded hills of the Swabian Jura in the north. This was a good place to make a camp, with fresh water nearby and forage for horses and mules plentiful in the neighbourhood. It might also be a good place to fight, provided that preparations were made in good time. The plain of Höchstädt was certainly well suited for mounted operations, and this would please the French, with their numerous cavalry, very well. Also, as an added comfort, the boggy Nebel stream ran straight across the plain, and shielded the Franco-Bavarian encampment from any sudden attack; and so there the army stayed, setting up their massed lines of tents on 12 August.

Tallard did, at first, intend to dam the Nebel stream, to increase the marshy obstacle, and also to erect a redan in the centre of his camp and man it with artillery. The Elector asked him not to do either, wanting to protect the still unharvested crops of his own farmers. Thinking it of no real importance, the Marshal agreed to the request and the ground remained undisturbed. The Comte de Merode-Westerloo, a wittily observant Walloon officer serving with Tallard, described the area occupied by their armies:

> *Our right wing was on the left bank of the River Danube with the village of Blenheim some two hundred yards to its front. All the generals of the right wing had quarters there. In front of this village ran a small stream* [Nebel], *running from its source a mile away to the left...The Elector and his men held a position reaching as far as the village of Lutzingen, which contained his headquarters, with the woods stretching away towards Nordlingen to his front. Before this position was an area of marshy ground, a few hamlets and one or two mills along the little stream. Blenheim village itself was surrounded by hedges; fences and other obstacles enclosed gardens and meadows. All in all the position was pretty fair, but had we advanced a mere eight hundred or a thousand paces farther to our front we would have held a far more compact position, with our right still on the Danube and our left protected by woods.*

The Comte (although speaking with the valuable benefit of hindsight) was absolutely right. A more serious omission by the

Marlborough looks out from Tapfheim church tower.

Marshals and the Elector could not be conceived, than to apparently give no thought to holding the village of Schwenningen, lying about a half a mile in advance of the Franco-Bavarian encampment. Here the wooded hills and the Danube river were no more than one mile apart, instead of the four miles that they had to cover on the plain.

While the French and Bavarians snuggled into their seemingly safe camp, Marlborough and Eugene, with 52,000 men and 60 guns, were marching steadily towards them, shielded by the outcropping wooded hills, through the villages of Münster and Tapfheim. In the afternoon of 12 August, the two commanders went to a small hill near the hamlet of Wolperstetten, and then ascended the picturesque tower of the church at Tapfheim to view the enemy camp. To their delight they could plainly see that the

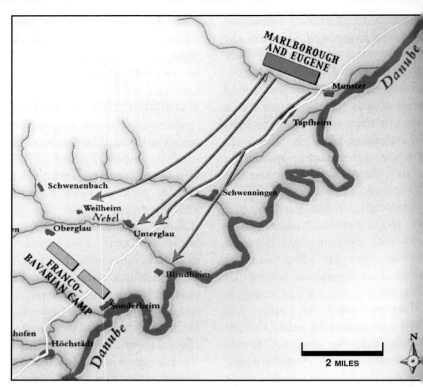

Marlborough forces the Schwenningen defile to attack the French and Bavarians, 12–13 August 1704.

tent-lines were being laid out a few miles away on the firm ground of the plain of Höchstädt, rather than in the less comfortable, but more secure, marshy ground near that town itself. Captain Robert Parker wrote afterwards:

> *Here was a fine plain without a hedge or ditch for the cavalry on both sides to show their bravery.*

Although Parker seemed to overlook the presence of the Nebel stream, he was right in that the open plain beyond the obstacle was excellent cavalry country.

The whole of 12 August was alive with alarms and skirmishes as the outposts and scouts of the two armies brushed against each other. The Duc d'Humieres, one of Tallard's cavalry commanders, was sufficiently concerned to send forward the Marquis de Silly with a detachment of forty squadrons of cavalry and dragoons to find out what the Allies were doing. These were driven off by Archibald Rowe's brigade of British infantry, who deployed to cover the pioneers of the advancing army, labouring to bridge the streams in the area and improve the crude forest tracks leading

52

westwards to Höchstädt. Marlborough wrote that: 'Intelligence was brought that the enemy's squadrons had attempted to fall on our workmen, but had been repulsed by the guard which covered them.' It was not quite that easy, as de Silly's troopers were a tough and inquisitive lot, and the 1st English Foot Guards had to go to Rowe's assistance before the unwelcome French attention was dealt with. Marlborough then moved quickly to secure the narrow strip of land between the marshy Danube and the wooded Fuchsberg hill, at the Schwenningen defile. Rowe's British Brigade, the 1st English Foot Guards and Wilkes's Hessian brigade occupied the village that evening as dusk fell.

The seizure of this important tactical ground virtually without any real fighting was a significant achievement for Marlborough. Had Tallard manned the village of Schwenningen, he would have had to fight on a very narrow frontage compared with that on the plain of Höchstädt. The simple reason for this oversight is that neither of the French or Bavarian commanders expected to have to fight here at all. Numerically superior, and with the apparently certain knowledge that time was against their opponent, they appeared to be mesmerised by the prospect that the Duke would lamely abandon his campaign, and take the prudent course – to withdraw along his lines of supply into Franconia. Prisoners taken by de Silly's cavalry, when questioned, supposed that their army was about to withdraw. In the meantime, the French and Bavarians could occupy their comfortable camp, with flanks secured by the Danube on the one hand and the hills of the Jura on the other, while awaiting developments and watching for a chance to strike at any clumsy move their opponents might make.

That night, Marlborough's army lay in the woods near to Schwenningen, just across the Fuchsberg hill from the plain of Höchstädt. The soldiers slept in the open that Saturday night, under brilliant stars, while in the French and Bavarian camp the troops relaxed in their tents, entirely ignorant of the calamity that was to befall them the following day. The Comte de Merode-Westerloo, who had tried to take part in the skirmishing that afternoon, remembered:

Filled with curiosity to discover how events were faring, I rode out beyond Blindheim village into the corn-filled plain – taking good care not to get too far away from any escort, which I might well have needed. When I saw our troops falling back I also returned to the camp, and sat down to a good plate of

*soup in Blindheim along with my generals and colonels. I was
never in better form, and after wining and dining well, we one
and all dispersed to our respective quarters. I had placed my
Spanish [Walloon] troops under the Duc d'Humieres away on
the left [of Tallard's Wing], slightly in rear of my position. I
was personally in command of the right wing of the second
line. I don't believe I ever slept sounder than on that night.*

Captain Parker wrote of the intervening dark hours:

*We lay on our arms all night and next day, being the 2
August [O.S.], we marched by break of day.*

The drum rolls that called the sleepy soldiers stiffly to their feet
could be heard in the French and Bavarian camp, but seemed to
cause no alarm. Remarkably, that very morning, Tallard spent a
few minutes on rising in dictating a letter to his private secretary,
to send to Louis XIV in Versailles. In a memorable passage the
Marshal predicted that the Allied campaign was, in effect, check-
mated, and that it was expected that the Duke's army would
withdraw northwards towards Nordlingen and Franconia before
very long:

*It looks as if they will march this day. Rumour in the
countryside expects them at Nordlingen. If that be true, they
will leave us between the Danube and themselves and in
consequence they will have difficulty in sustaining the posts
and depots which they have taken in Bavaria.*

How wrong the French Marshal was, with his simple inability to
grasp the intrepid characters of both Marlborough and Eugene.
So confident were the French and Bavarians, that orders were
even posted that foragers should go out as usual that morning.
Tallard was a good soldier and so too were his fellow
commanders, but their neglectful complacency and disdain for
the vigour and daring of their opponents was soon to be seen.

Marlborough's plan for battle was simple, but very demanding.
To get at the French and Bavarians he had to move out onto a
wide plain, in open view and within cannon range of the enemy,
and deploy his army on a four-mile wide front, then force a
passage of the boggy Nebel stream. It was too much to hope that
he could do all this unopposed. However, the way in which his
opponents lay in their camp indicated to the Duke that they would
take some time to draw up in proper battle array themselves. In
this he was proved quite correct, and the Duke planned to use this
valuable pause to deploy onto the plain of Höchstädt and force the

Marlborough writing his orders in his coach, by R. Caton Woodville.

Blindheim church tower. The French and Bavarian commanders viewed Marlborough's deployment from here.

line of the stream, before Tallard, Marsin and the Elector could properly react to his advance.

It was Tallard's Wing on the French and Bavarian right that was to be the target of the attack launched by the Duke of Marlborough, although this can only have been fully confirmed in the Duke's mind as the events of the day unfolded. After taking the Sacrament from Dr Hare, he then conferred closely with Dubislaw Natzmer while sitting in his coach at the roadside, as the marching columns of the army filed past in the early morning light. This Prussian officer had been defeated on the very same ground only the previous year and knew the area well as a result. The British and German soldiers who had held Schwenningen through the night joined the march, making a ninth column on the left of the army, while the artillery made good use of the main road leading from Donauwörth. The Duke undoubtedly had the outline of his attack in his mind as his army moved onto the plain, for the terrain here was open and gently rolling, once the Nebel stream was passed. Assessing this as his army marched onwards, and the French and Bavarian camp came into view, Marlborough's unfolding plan was to deploy his own cavalry on the left to crush Tallard in the open, while Eugene pinned down Marsin and the Elector on the right. John Deane of the 1st English Foot Guards wrote in his journal:

August the 2nd [13th N.S.] *the Generall beat at 2 a clock in the morning; and there halted till a little; and then marched and approached the enemy about 6 and as soon as ever the*

enemy get sight of us they fired there great guns uppon us but
we played none at them till 9 a clock in the morning.

Eugene was directed, with the smaller Wing of the Allied army
(about 20,000 men and 20 guns), to move across the face of the
French and Bavarian position, with his left flank possibly exposed
to harassing fire, and attack the Bavarians in the area of
Lutzingen. If this assault was pressed with enough vigour, and
Eugene could be depended on in that respect, then the Elector
and Marsin would have no time or troops to spare to aid Tallard
on the right. However, the ground which Eugene had to cross was
marshy and cut up with small streams, and patches of scrub
impeded progress. Not only would the Prince have to throw out
flank guards in case of attacks from Marsin's troops, but his
artillery would find the going difficult, and would take time to get
into position.

As Marlborough's marching columns poured out past
Schwenningen onto the approaches to the plain of Höchstädt, at
least one of Tallard's officers was thoroughly alarmed. The Comte
de Merode-Westerloo was just then sleepily awakening from his
night's gentle slumber in Blindheim village. The Comte tells us:

I slept deeply until six in the morning when I was abruptly
awakened by one of my old retainers – the head groom in fact
– who rushed into the barn all out of breath. He had just
returned from taking my horses out to grass at four in the
morning. This fellow, LeFranc, shook me awake and blurted
out that the enemy was there. Thinking to mock him I asked
'Where? There?' and he at once replied, 'Yes – there – there' –
flinging wide as he spoke the door of the barn and drawing my
bed-curtains. The door opened straight on to the fine, sunlit
plain beyond – and the whole area appeared to be covered by
enemy squadrons.

Hurriedly dressing, the Comte called his squadrons to attention
and started to draw them up in a kind of order, amid the
paraphernalia of their camp, while the rest of the army were still
shaking themselves awake. Tallard hurried past at one point, and
commended the Comte for his vigour. Signal guns were fired to
bring in foraging parties and picquets, and all was hustle and
bustle in the camps as the French and Bavarian troops tried to
draw up into battle order to face the unexpected threat. The guns
were heard by the Margrave of Baden, in his headquarters tent
before Ingolstadt some forty miles to the east. He added a

sentence to a letter that he was just then writing to Emperor Leopold in Vienna: 'The Prince and the Duke are engaged today to the westward. Heaven bless them.'

The two Marshals and the Elector hurried to the church tower in Blindheim village from where they could view the Allied deployment on the far side of the Nebel stream. Tactically on the back foot, they held a hurried council of war as the enemy columns grew longer and longer before their very eyes. It was plain that little time was available to deploy their forces in effective battle formation, for the manner in which their troops had gone into the comfortable camp was not an ideal arrangement from which to fight an active and dangerous enemy who might soon have them by the throat.

The Nebel stream ran across the plain of Höchstädt and provided a significant obstacle against any direct attack on the camp. In 1704, without benefit of modern drainage, the wide brook was boggy and the banks treacherous underfoot, capable of being waded by infantrymen certainly, but only with difficulty. The Marshals and the Elector viewed the growing masses of troops across the stream, and debated how they should hold the precious water barrier against the coming assault. Marsin felt it best to close his infantry right up to the stream itself, and force the attackers to pay a dear price for every yard gained. Tallard, however, was intent on using his cavalry to best effect, and they could not operate very well in the marshy grass at the water's edge. He declared his intention to hold his troops back from the stream, on the higher ground of the plain. Once Marlborough's army had crossed the water and was in place, he would throw his powerful cavalry into the attack and drive the Allies to destruction in the stream at their back. The Elector, mindful of the catastrophe at the Schellenberg, cautioned Tallard 'Beware of these troops [the British], they are very dangerous.'

This was a sensible enough tactic for Tallard to adopt, provided that his infantry, artillery and cavalry were used in close co-operation. However, it also allowed Marlborough the chance to get across the Nebel stream without serious interference, and this was a necessary preliminary to the very kind of battle the Duke had in mind. The two Marshals could not agree the best course, so each went their own tactical way. Given numerical superiority, and the natural strength of their position, neither commander was necessarily wrong, but the lack of a common approach was risky and, as will be seen, that vital co-operation between the arms in Tallard's Wing was soon to go adrift. However, at Tallard's request, Marsin did agree to detach sixteen squadrons of cavalry to his support on the open cornfields between Oberglau and Blindheim, despite the risk to the horses of contagion from glanders. Tallard responded by sending two of his infantry battalions to help garrison Oberglau.

Despite their surprise at having to fight a battle at all, Tallard, Marsin and the Elector made their preparations with competent skill. The villages on either flank of the position, Lutzingen in the north and Blindheim to the south, were occupied by infantry. The cottages were loop-holed for muskets, and carts, furniture, barn doors, logs and debris were piled up as barricades in the entrances to the narrow alleyways. Fields of fire were good, although Blindheim was partially bounded by orchards and allotment fences. The open cornfields all around permitted fairly good observation, but the standing wheat hampered the most advantageous siting of the French batteries. With no system of forward observers for artillery at that time, the gunners would not have been allowed to waste expensive round-shot by firing blindly through the crops. At least one six-gun battery, near Blindheim village, got around this problem by firing obliquely across the slope at Marlborough's infantry gathering near Unterglau. This hamlet, alongside the Nebel stream, was set alight by the French, as Weilheim Farm had been, to hamper Marlborough's deployment. Merode-Westerloo wrote that two small water mills close to Blindheim, where the Nebel stream divided into two to form a small reedy islet, were also put to the torch. Robert Parker, however, remembers that these were set on fire during the course of the battle, as the French soldiers stationed there abandoned them.

In Lutzingen, Count Maffei, veteran of the Schellenberg fight six weeks earlier, deployed just five Bavarian infantry battalions (some reports say twelve but this computation actually includes the French battalions placed in the woods beyond the village). On the edge of the village a great battery of sixteen guns was established on a slight rise. From here an excellent field of fire was had across the lush cornfields and the Nebel stream towards Weilheim Farm, where Eugene's Danish and Prussian infantry were gradually taking up position, and could clearly be seen in the morning sunlight. To the left, in the wooded hills beyond

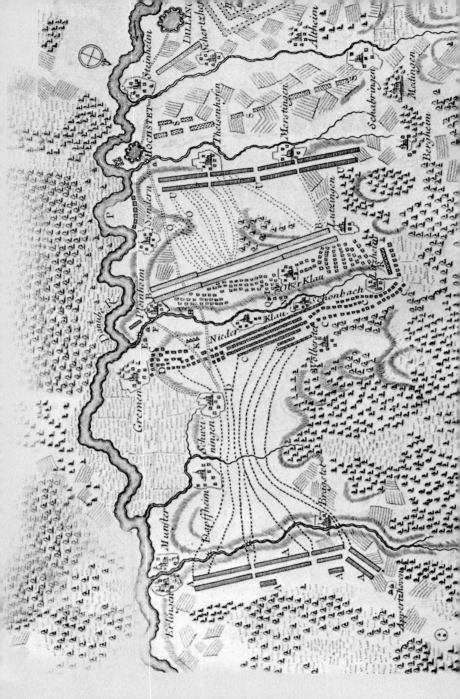

An eighteenth-century map depicting the battle of Blenheim. The narrow defile at Schwenningen is clearly shown.

Lutzingen, seven French infantry battalions under the Marquis de Rozel were moving into place, to anchor the French and Bavarian line firmly there. Between Lutzingen and Oberglau, the Elector deployed his twenty-seven squadrons of cavalry. Count D'Arco was in command of fourteen squadrons of Bavarian cavalry, while Count Wolframsdorf had thirteen more in support nearby. To their right, in the open overlooking the stream, stood Marsin's forty squadrons of French cavalry and twelve battalions of infantry. Oberglau was turned into a strongpoint and packed with fourteen battalions of French and émigré Irish infantry under the Marquis de Blainville (son of the great naval and financial reformer, Colbert.) Six powerful batteries were ranged alongside the village, to cover the approaches from Unterglau and Weilheim Farm.

On the right of the French and Bavarian position, Tallard deployed sixty-four squadrons of French and Walloon cavalry on the plain of Höchstädt, leading gently down towards the Nebel stream. The slope would give impetus to their charge, when it came. Nine battalions of young French infantry stood near the Höchstädt road in their support, although these soldiers' lack of experience might mean they were not as steady as was needed. On the cornfield next to Blindheim, where the garrison was in the charge of the Marquis de Clerambault, were the three battalions from the Régiment du Roi, and nine battalions of infantry occupied the village itself. A further four battalions stood to the rear, and eleven more were on the higher ground of the plain, ready to move forward when their support was needed. This was a strong position, made more so by twelve squadrons of dismounted dragoons, who threw up a sketchy breastwork in the marshy grass leading the few hundred yards from the village to the edge of the Danube itself.

Once properly shaken out, the French and Bavarian army occupied a generally good position. The wide Danube shielded their right, and on this flank the strongpoint village of Blindheim was held by a numerous garrison under a veteran and skilful commander. On the other side of the plain of Höchstädt, Lutzingen was similarly fortified and occupied by seasoned Bavarian troops, with a powerful battery in support. The wooded hills to the left of the village thronged with French infantry, so that flank was also well held. The boggy Nebel stream protected the whole wide frontage of the army, and Oberglau, almost, but not quite, in the centre of the line, was packed with infantry. The French and Bavarian batteries were drawn up to cover the Nebel, although getting good points of observation remained a problem in places, and the guns around the villages, Blindheim and Oberglau in particular, were too far apart to achieve effective overlapping fire. The problem was less acute between Lutzingen and Oberglau. The numerous squadrons of cavalry were drawn up on the rising ground above the stream, and, all things considered, by about 11am that day, the Elector, Tallard and Marsin could feel that they had recovered their poise quite well, and were ready to fight. Their position, on the face of it, was sufficiently strong and the army so well posted that many prudent commanders might not have attempted an attack at all. The Duke's chaplain, Dr Hare, said afterwards 'Almost all the generals were against my Lord's attacking the enemy, they thought it so difficult', and Earl Orkney, a highly proficient and aggressive infantry commander who fought under Marlborough at Blenheim that day, wrote:

> *I confess that it is entirely owing to my Lord Duke, for I declare, had I been asked to give my opinion, I had been against it, considering the ground where they had been camped and the strength of the army. But his Grace knew the necessity there was of a battle.*

On the Allied side of the Nebel stream matters progressed rather unevenly. With the shorter distance to march, and firm going underfoot, Marlborough's British, Dutch, Danish and German troops got into place fairly quickly, moving up on either side of smouldering Unterglau. The Duke promptly set his pioneers to bridging the stream; those rudimentary farm bridges that had existed had been torn down by the French picquets as they pulled back after setting Unterglau alight. In all, five of these makeshift causeways were constructed that morning, using 700 fascines cut the previous evening in the woods on the Fuchsberg hill, and the marshy banks were levelled in places to allow the Allied troops easy passage. While this went on the French artillery near to Blindheim fired on the growing ranks of Marlborough's troops, and a round-shot struck the ground underneath the belly of Marlborough's distinctive grey horse, showering mount and rider with dust. The Duke calmly looked around and suggested to his brother, Charles Churchill, who commanded his infantry that day, that the troops should lie down, both to gain shelter from the

French gunners, and from the warm sun. Orkney wrote:

His Grace rode along the lines to observe the posture and countenances of his men, and found them and the officers of all nations of the Allies very cheerful and impatient of coming to a closer engagement with the enemy. And, as he was passing in front of the first line a large cannon ball from one of the enemy's batteries grazed upon the ploughed land, close by his horse's side, and almost covered him with dust.

Marlborough then dismounted to take refreshment with his officers, before ordering that divine service should be held at the head of each regiment. The soldiers knelt in the dust while the regimental chaplains prayed over the piled drums and regimental colours; still the French guns thundered away. 'A heavy cannonade was opened from every part of the enemy's [French] right wing.'

Eugene's troops, by comparison, struggled to get into place in good time; the ground did not make for rapid marching, and flank guards had to be placed to watch for interference from Marsin's troops: 'Great difficulty occurred in bringing up the artillery, for the ground being extremely broken.' As the morning wore on Marlborough became anxious for news; too much time was being allowed his opponents, and the precious tactical advantage snatched with his daring advance to the plain of Höchstädt could be lost if they took the initiative and moved to the attack. At midday the Duke sent William Cadogan to enquire after Eugene's progress. Reassured that the Prince was getting into place, albeit slowly, the Duke ordered the bands of the army to strike up, both to cheer the soldiers as they patiently waited under the French fire, and to intimidate their opponents. The French bands responded and a musical duel began across the plain of Höchstädt as the musicians of each army sought to outshine the other. Marlborough's gunners were in action too, having been placed by the Duke himself to ensure good fields of fire, and Merode-Westerloo wrote that one of his favourite horses was a casualty of the Allied fire during this phase of the battle (he lost thirteen mounts in all that day). 'I was riding past Forsac's regiment when a shot carried away the head of my horse and killed two troopers.' Despite this, the Comte could not fail to be impressed by the martial glory of the scene that unfolded across the plain:

It would be impossible to imagine a more magnificent spectacle, the two armies in full array were so close to one another that they exchanged fanfares of trumpet calls and rolls of kettledrums. The brightest imaginable sun shone down on the two armies drawn up in the plain. You could even distinguish the uniforms of each successive unit; a number of generals and aides de camp galloped here and there; all in all, it was an almost indescribably stirring sight.

At last, at about 12.30pm, a message came from Eugene that his cavalry and infantry were in place opposite Lutzingen and would go in on the Duke's command; 'The joyful news that Eugene was ready.' The Imperial artillery on the Allied right was still struggling across the broken ground and was not in action, but Eugene would attack anyway. The Allied soldiers were called to their feet, the foot soldiers checked their dressing under the barked commands of their sergeants, the cavalry took to their saddles, and to the blaring of trumpets and the tapping of drums the battle began.

Allied artillery in action. Detail from the Blenheim Tapestry. By kind permission of His Grace the Duke of Marlborough.

The Duke of Marlborough with his staff officers, awaiting the submission of Marshal Tallard on the field of battle.

Blenheim Palace Tapestry. By kind permission of His Grace the Duke of Marlborough.

Kit Welsh or Christian Davies. The adventurous female dragoon fought with the Scots Greys at Schellenberg and Blenheim, and was wounded in 1706 at Ramillies.
Author's collection.

William, 1st Earl Cadogan, Marlborough's dependable Quartermaster-General and close friend. He was Master-General of the Ordnance from 1722 onwards.
Author's collection.

John Churchill, 1st Duke of Marlborough, with his Chief Engineer, Colonel John Armstrong. Armstrong is holding a plan of the fortifications of Bouchain. Artist Enoch Seaman. By kind permission of His Grace the Duke of Marlborough.

The 1st English Foot Guards struggle across the Nebel stream to attack Blindheim village. The vulnerability of the troops at this stage is evident, an interesting comparison with the well-ordered march to action shown by Simkin.
Laguerre oil-sketch. By kind permission of the Marquis of Anglesey.

The British infantry approach Blindheim village. One of a series produced so that individual regiments could have their own colours portrayed, in this case Ferguson's/The Cameronians. Artist Richard Simkin. Author's collection

Prince Eugene (Eugen) of Savoy

François-Eugene de Savoie-Carignan, Prince of the House of Savoy, was born in October 1663 in Paris, the son of Eugene-Maurice, Comte de Soissons, and Olympe Mancini, the niece of Cardinal Mazarin. Refused a commission in the French army by King Louis XIV (who thought he would make a good priest instead), Eugene absconded at the age of twenty to the Spanish Netherlands. Travelling on to Vienna he entered the service of the Holy Roman Empire. He fought against the Turks at the relief of Vienna, and in Hungary where he was appointed Imperial commander. At the battle of Zenta (1697) Eugene destroyed a major Turkish army and his reputation as a general was made for all time.

Appointed to the Imperial War Council in 1703, Eugene met the Duke of Marlborough for the first time in 1704, and the two men became close friends. They campaigned successfully together, most notably at Blenheim, Oudenarde (1708) and Malplaquet (1709). Eugene was also the victor at the battle of Turin (1706) where the French Marshal Marsin was killed, but he was less successful in the abortive campaign against the French naval base at Toulon in 1707.

After the Treaty of Utrecht (1713) Eugene continued to lead the Imperial armies against the French along the Rhine. At the Peace of Rastatt (1714)

Prince Eugene of Savoy by Kneller, painted in London in 1712.

he was appointed the Imperial Governor of the Austrian (previously Spanish) Netherlands. Campaigning once again against the Turks, Eugene won battles at Peterwardin (1716) and the capture of Belgrade (1717).

Although the Prince retired from campaigning to become principal adviser to the Emperor, he was appointed as the Imperial commander in the War of the Polish Succession in 1734–1735, despite rapidly failing health. A lifelong bachelor (although fond of women) Eugene was a noted patron of the arts. He died in his sleep at his home in Vienna in April 1736.

Chapter 5

THE FIGHT FOR THE VILLAGES

A T 1PM ON 13 AUGUST 1704 Marlborough sent word to Lord John Cutts to press forward with his column of infantry and storm the village of Blindheim on the banks of the Danube. At the same time Prince Eugene was requested to assault Lutzingen on the Allied right flank. In this way the Duke intended that the French and Bavarian infantry would be ruthlessly tied down and unable to take part in the crucial cavalry battle on the wide plain of Höchstädt. Dr Hare wrote that the Allied troops were: 'All advancing cheerfully showed a firm and glad countenance and seeming to be confident.'

Cutts (described by Jonathan Swift as being as brave and brainless as the sword at his side, and known popularly as 'the Salamander' for his liking of being in the hottest fire) gave the word and Archibald Rowe's British brigade rose quietly from the edge of the Nebel stream, where they had been sheltering, and stepped forward across the boggy ground to the enemy bank. Clambering up the gentle slope that leads towards the edge of Blindheim, they had some cover from the dip in the ground formed by the stream, and their approach was unhindered, apart from the French battery which fired on them from the slightly higher ground at the edge of the village. Simultaneously, John Ferguson's British brigade, led by the 1st English Foot Guards, shook out to the left of Rowe's men. They headed for a long line of overturned carts running from the cottages to the marshy edge of the Danube. This barricade was manned by dismounted French dragoons from the Notat, La Reine and Maitre de Camp Régiments under command of the Comte d'Hautefeuille. The dressing of the ranks of the British regiments was aligned, regimental colours snapped smartly in the breeze, and the two brigades went into the attack. John Deane remembered the approach well:

About 3 a clock in the afternoon our English on the left was ordered by My Lord Duke to attacque a village on the left full of French called Blenheim which village they had fortified and made so vastly strong and barackaded so fast wth trees, planks,

A near contemporary view of the Battle of Blenheim, 1704.

> *coffers, chests, wagons, carts and palisades that it was almost*
> *an impossibility to think which way to get into it.*

During the British advance, the discipline of the French was superb. Apart from the fire of the battery on the edge of Blindheim, the approach was met with ominous silence from the defenders. James Campbell, who took part in the attack with Rowe's Regiment (subsequently the Royal Scots Fusiliers), wrote home two days later:

> *We went throu the watter that was upon their front with*
> *little opposition and touck ane piece of cannon after that we*
> *mead a little halt and attacked the village that was upon their*
> *right called Blindheim.*

As the range closed, steady volleys of musketry poured out from the French barricades, and many in the leading ranks of attackers tumbled down in the blast. Rowe had ordered his men not to return fire until he could touch the breastworks at the village, and as he stepped forward to strike an overturned cart with his sword, he was shot through the thigh and fell, mortally wounded. Behind him his men closed up the gaps torn in their ranks and rushed forward to exchange shots and bayonet thrusts with the defenders. Two officers, Lieutenant-Colonel Dalyell and Major Campbell, ran over to recover Rowe's body, but they too were killed. James Campbell goes on:

> They received us with so hot a fire that they killed or wounded twenty officers our Brigadier is mortally wounded and his leg brock which is regretted by the whole armie.

Between the village and river, the Foot Guards moved forward into a small orchard and were met with heavy volleys from the French dragoons. Colonel Philip Dormer was mortally wounded and the huge regimental colour of the Guards was 'All shott to pieces'. Soon Ferguson's men recoiled from the terrible fire, and like Rowe's brigade, they had to fall back towards the Nebel to recover their shaken order.

At this dangerous moment, with Cutts's attack faltering, eight squadrons (sixteen companies) of the elite French Gens d'Armes, commanded by the veteran Swiss officer Beat-Jacques von Zurlauben, came sweeping in massed ranks effortlessly across the slope from the plain of Höchstädt. They cut in at the exposed flank of the right-hand British battalion – Rowe's own regiment, whose ranks were ragged and the officers flustered. Now, von Zurlauben's troopers, resplendent in their laced red coats, rode furiously among them, cutting and slashing with their long swords. The soldiers tried frantically to form square but instead broke apart, the colour ensign fell and the regimental colour was lost to an exultant gendarme.

Wilkes's Hessian brigade was nearby, lying in the marshy grass at the water's edge. They rose to their feet and moved resolutely forward to steady the stricken British regiment. Their

A panoramic view of the plain of Höchstädt looking westwards from just west of Blindheim across French and Bavarian positions.

Jura hills

disciplined volleys, described as 'a peal of fire', and glistening bayonets drove off the Gens d'Armes, who were themselves now in some disarray after their impetuous charge. The lost colour was dropped and returned safely to the regiment, while Cutts gathered his battered troops into line, ready for a fresh effort. Gallantly the British and Hessian troops advanced towards the barricades again, but the French fire was unfaltering and the attackers' casualties were again severe. They were thrown back towards the Nebel stream once again, without the satisfaction of making any impression at all on the defenders of Blindheim village.

The ardour with which the Allied attack was mounted had its effect however, as Clerambault grew increasingly nervous at the scale of the assault. He began to draw into the village all those French infantry battalions standing to the side and rear, in the cornfields and gardens. These units had been placed where they could move to support either the garrison in Blindheim or, more importantly perhaps, the French cavalry in their vital battle on the plain of Höchstädt. So distracted did Clerambault become under the remorseless pressure exerted by Cutts, that it seems he suffered some form of nervous breakdown that hot day. He went distractedly from one part of the village to another, questioning his officers, apparently unable to decide on what to do for the best. As the afternoon wore on he gradually packed twenty-seven infantry battalions and de Hautefille's twelve squadrons of dismounted dragoons, perhaps 12,000 men in all, into the narrow streets and walled churchyard of Blindheim.

It soon became plain that the garrison in Blindheim was so strong that no attack by the Allied troops available on this flank, at that stage in the day, could hope to succeed. Marlborough had

Trees mark line of Nebel stream

Allied deployment beyond tree line

Fore and middle ground: French and Bavarian deployment

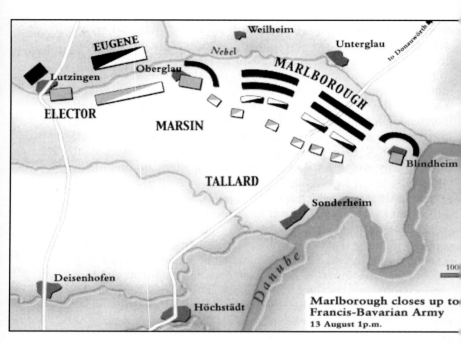

Marlborough closes up to
Francis-Bavarian Army
13 August 1p.m.

just ridden over from near Unterglau to confer with Cutts. The
Duke countermanded Cutts's declared intention to attack the
barricades again, asking him just to keep Clerambault and his
garrison occupied, while the battle was won on another part of the
field. Robert Parker of the Royal Irish Regiment said that the
British infantry:

> Soon rallied, returned to the charge, and drove the enemy
> from the skirts of the village. They had not the room to draw
> up in any manner of order, or even make use of their arms.
> Thereupon we drew up in great order about 80 paces from
> them, from where we made several vain attempts to break in
> upon them, in which many brave men were lost to no purpose.
> It was not possible for them to rush upon us in a disorderly
> manner without running upon the very points of our bayonets.
> This great body of [French] troops was of no further use to
> Tallard, being obliged to keep on the defensive.

The success of the attack on Blindheim was such that no more
than about 5,000 British and Hessian soldiers penned more than
twice that number of French infantry and dragoons to the
defences of the place, helplessly unable to assist Tallard's cavalry

in their vital battle nearby. Whenever the French infantry attempted a sortie they faced the remorseless musketry of the British and Hessian regiments ranged alongside the village, sweeping the narrow exits between the cottages with a murderous fire: 'we mowed them down with our platoons' Robert Parker wrote afterwards. Holcroft Blood had also had a brace of guns manhandled across the Nebel to support the infantry.

At the same time that Cutts attacked Blindheim, the Prince of Anhalt-Dessau (the 'Old Dessauer' of Frederick the Great's wars) led forward four brigades of Danish and Prussian infantry against Lutzingen next to the wooded hills on the other flank. This was a well fortified place, the Bavarian infantry had all morning to arrange their defences, and the great battery on the edge of the village enjoyed a good field of fire across the open ground stretching to the small hamlet of Schwennenbach, near to the wood-line, and Weilheim Farm. The attacking infantry came on in good order across cornfields almost too perfectly open and even. The Nebel stream here, although boggy and broken into numerous small creeks, was no particular obstacle, and it was crossed without great effort. As soon as Anhalt-Dessau's infantry reached the far bank however, they were struck by heavy volleys of musketry from Maffei's infantry, and salvoes of canister from the Bavarian guns, both in front of the village and placed in enfilade on the wood-line to the right. Terrible gaps were torn in the attacking ranks, but the Prussians rallied, pressed forward, and attempted to storm into the great battery. Meanwhile, the Danes under Count Scholten, tormented by fire from their right flank, turned to drive the

French infantryman, c. 1704, Tournasis Regiment.

French infantry out of the copses beyond the village.

While this desperate struggle went on, Eugene's first line cavalry under the Imperial General of Horse, Prince Maximilien of Hannover, picked its way across the Nebel stream. Hardly had the squadrons formed a hasty line on the drier ground than Marsin's French cavalry and their Bavarian comrades came teeming forward to engage them. In a brief hacking contest, this counter-attack was held by the Imperial horsemen, and then thrown back. The second line of Marsin's squadrons came forward to the attack and the Prince's cavalry now lost order and scrambled back across the Nebel in considerable confusion. This move uncovered the left flank of the Prussians as they struggled to retain a hold on the great battery. Threatened with envelopment, two of Anhalt-Dessau's battalions scattered and the Prussian infantry had to fall hurriedly back. As they did so the Danes found in their turn that their left flank was exposed, and they also had to withdraw. The Allied infantry attempted to make a stand but were pursued so vigorously by Count D'Arco's Bavarian Life Guards that some panic did take hold as Eugene's troops scrambled back across the Nebel stream. Ten infantry colours were lost to the Bavarians, and hundreds of prisoners were taken. John Deane wrote of the affair:

> Prince Eujeane commanded the right wing that day and made a bold attacque upon the enemy and the enemy did as bravely stand itt and so stoutly behave themselves that Prince Eujeane was forced to give way.

Eugene was only able to rally his shaken cavalry and infantry on the wood-line at the foot of the Waldberg near Schwennenbach, well beyond their starting point. Before long, his commanders had re-ordered their ranks and they came into the attack once more, led by the second-line squadrons under the Duke of Württemberg-Teck, forcing their way at heavy cost back across the Nebel. They were caught in a murderous cross-fire of artillery from the Bavarians in Lutzingen and Marsin's batteries near to Oberglau, and were again thrown back in disarray. The Elector attempted to follow up this success with a stinging counter-attack, but his troopers responded rather lamely. The French and Bavarians on this part of the field were almost as disordered as their opponents, their horses were tired and their losses had not been light. For some time the opposing commanders had to look mostly to restore their soldiers' fighting zeal; the opposing lines

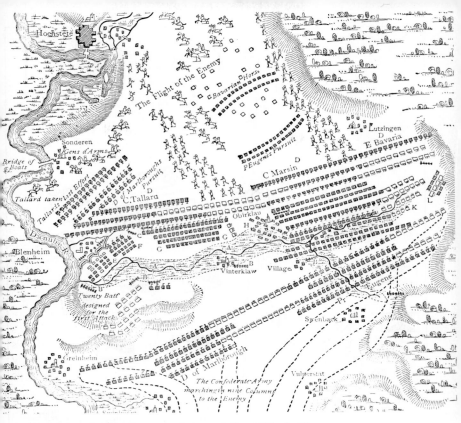

An evocative nineteenth century interpretation of the battle.

drew close to each other, but did not engage. Dr Hare saw both Eugene and the Elector vigorously exhorting and encouraging their men for fresh efforts: 'The Elector of Bavaria was seen riding up and down, and inspiring the men also with fresh courage.'

While Eugene's horsemen flagged, Anhalt-Dessau's Danish and Prussian infantry again stormed into Lutzingen, and the wooded copses nearby. Fighting the French and Bavarians in desperate stabbing, clubbing, hand-to-hand combat, the Dessauer's men could not sustain this second attack without proper support, and fell back again across the mud of the stream to recover. Maffei's infantry, shaken by the ferocity of the assault, did not pursue this time.

With great effort Marlborough's plan, sketched out in his mind at the Tapfheim church the previous afternoon, and formed into full detail as his army moved through the Schwenningen defile

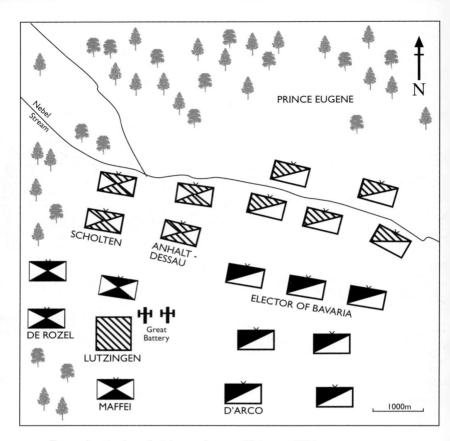

Eugene's attack on Lutzingen, 2pm on 13 August 1704.

towards the plain of Höchstädt, was taking effect. He had thrown heavy infantry attacks against both of his opponents' flanks and, although these had been repulsed, the French and Bavarian commanders were engrossed in these important but subsidiary actions. They had no freedom of manoeuvre, only Marlborough retained that, for Tallard's cavalry, the centre of gravity of the whole French and Bavarian army, was now devoid of proper support and exposed to assault by superior forces on the open plain. To this ripe target the Duke now turned his attention.

While Clerambault was packing the precious French infantry into Blindheim village, Marlborough in contrast began to move infantry away from Cutts, towards the centre of the battlefield; they had a role to play in the great battle to be fought there. Hulsen's Hessian and Hanoverian brigade (commanded on the day by Colonel St Paul) and Hamilton's brigade of British troops were moved to support Charles Churchill's advance. Soon afterwards the dismounted dragoon regiments of Hay and Ross were also detached from Cutts and marched towards the centre of the field, and ten British squadrons of cavalry under Henry Lumley soon followed. These squadrons were moved forward across the stream into position to cover Cutts's right flank.

Despite the efforts of the French artillery under the Marquis de la Frequelière, Charles Churchill had got the Dutch, German and British infantry across the Nebel without very great delay, and they formed up in the cornfields facing the French cavalry massed on the plain of Höchstädt. The Allied cavalry followed and Marlborough's battle-line interlaced the cavalry with infantry in a novel manner, so that each arm could support the other. Also, the Duke took care to see that sufficient gaps were left

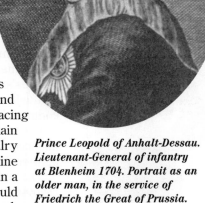

Prince Leopold of Anhalt-Dessau. Lieutenant-General of infantry at Blenheim 1704. Portrait as an older man, in the service of Friedrich the Great of Prussia. Artist not known.

between the infantry battalions so that his cavalry could pass and re-pass between their lines without hindrance, whether moving forward to the attack or retiring to recover their composure after a repulse.

The steady deployment of Marlborough's army did not go unchallenged by any means. As the Allied troops lined up on the approaches to the plain of Höchstädt, the Gens d'Armes under von Zurlauban came charging forward once again, looking to rout Lumley's British cavalry, who now linked Churchill's infantry with that of Cutts's column facing Blindheim. To split these two formations apart might seriously unbalance Marlborough's arrangements. As the squadrons of elite French cavalry came forward they were faced with five British squadrons under Colonel Frances Palmes. Although they had the advantage of the slope, the French squandered this by halting their advance to fire

French horse grenadier,
c.1704.

their carbines at the British troopers, before charging home. This antiquated and ineffective technique allowed Palmes time to throw a squadron outwards around each flank of the Gens d'Armes, who suddenly found themselves enveloped left and right, and were thrown back in terrible confusion. The gentlemen troopers then lost their nerve and galloped for the rear, careering through the ranks of those French infantry battalions that stood nearby to support them. Palmes attempted to follow up this initial success, but had to scramble his squadrons back in the face of musketry fire from infantry at the edge of Blindheim village, and fresh French cavalry that came cantering forward to oppose them. Palmes's men were driven back in some confusion and one of his squadron commanders, Major Richard Creed, was killed.

Creed's younger brother, John, tried unsuccessfully to save him and wrote to his mother three days later:

The enemy forst us to reteir & I missing my Dearest Brother un ye retreat I advanced in haste toards the enemys squadrons with indeavour to rescew him but a dismall sight found him strugling on ye ground & one of ye enemy over him with his sord in his hand I shot ye enemy and dismounted and lifted up my Brother and brught him off but he neaver spoke more.

Despite this rather scrambled recovery by the French, the startling and ignominious repulse of such supposedly elite cavalry as the Gens d'Armes had a significant effect. Consternation was felt throughout their army, and the Elector, on hearing the incredible news, said to an aide: 'What? Is it possible? The gentlemen of France fleeing? Go, tell them that I am here, in person. Rally them and lead them to the charge again.' Such stirring sentiments went for nothing as the officer sent with the message, the Marquis de Montigny-Langost, was taken prisoner a little later, while helping to rally the Gens d'Armes for a fresh effort:

> *I received two sabre cuts on the head, a sword thrust through the arm, a blow from a musket ball on the leg, and my horse was wounded. Thus, being surrounded on all sides with no hope of escape, I was taken by an officer, who taking away one of my pistols said to me 'I give you quarter, follow me and I will see your wounds dressed.'*

Having handed over his purse to his captor, the battered young Frenchman then escaped back to his own lines, as the Allied officer was wounded by a stray musket ball. The Marquis watched in exasperation as the ranks of Allied cavalry grew longer on the near side of the Nebel stream:

> *What a disappointment when I saw the English cavalry which had been repulsed returning to the charge, and again routing our Gendarmerie and the cavalry supporting them, and already crossing the* [Maulweyer] *stream and taking possession of our terrain.*

More tellingly, Tallard watched the flight of the Gens d'Armes in alarm, and rode across the field to confer with Marshal Marsin near to Oberglau. Tallard warned his colleague that the main threat was plainly on the far side of the Höchstädt road, and recommended that Marsin detach some of his army to reinforce the right Wing. The younger Marshal, who despite the fears of infection had already sent part of his cavalry to help Tallard earlier in the day, now refused. Eugene's second attack was still in full flood and, even if repulsed, would no doubt be renewed. Columns of Dutch and German infantry could be seen moving towards Oberglau, held by Marsin's own infantry, and Eugene's artillery was at last now getting into action. The Prince's gun-line was established at Weilheim Farm where fourteen pieces were placed, and from here a slight rise in the ground gave the Imperial gunners a good field of fire over which to pound the French position. So Marsin was under heavy pressure too, and Tallard must fight on alone.

While Tallard was engaged in anxious discussion with Marsin, his infantry were more and more being taken into Blindheim by the Marquis de Clerambault, who then compounded his mistake by ordering the Régiment du Roi, still standing on the cornfields, into the village too. The Marshal, fatally, did nothing to rectify his subordinate's folly as the afternoon wore on. Soon, all that Tallard had left to support his cavalry were the nine small battalions of young soldiers, standing near to the Höchstädt road, presumably too far away for Clerambault to get his hands on them. Robert Parker commented on the growing confusion that afflicted the French command that afternoon:

> *Tallard seeing his five* [eight] *squadrons so shamefully beaten by three* [plus the squadron thrown out by Palmes around either flank]*, was confounded to that degree, that he did not recover himself the whole day, for after that all his orders were given in a hurry and confusion.*

All this time the long lines of Marlborough's cavalry and infantry steadily grew on Tallard's side of the stream. Von Zurlauben tried several more times to disrupt them; his front-line cavalry squadrons darting forward down the gentle slope towards the Nebel. The effort lacked co-ordination and real power, and the coolly delivered volleys of the Allied infantry disconcerted the French horsemen. Not a lot was achieved, other than to further tire their horses, although at one point several Hanoverian and British squadrons were again temporarily thrown back on the left of the line. Von Bulow's Prussians stoutly rode forward to their aid, supported by the dragoons of Hay and Ross. The French cavalry withdrew a little, across the small Maulweyer stream, to recover their order and rest their mounts. The time was just after 3 in the afternoon, and soon afterwards the gallant and exhausted von Zurlauben was wounded in one of his cavalry's skirmishes with von Bulow's squadrons, and died two days later.

The Danish cavalry under command of the Duke of Württemberg (not to be confused with the Duke of Württemberg-Teck who fought with Eugene) had made slow work of getting over the Nebel stream, near to Oberglau. Marsin's infantry struck several times at their harassed ranks as the horsemen scrambled through the mud, and the Danes were initially driven back. Count Horn's Dutch infantry were nearby, and their volleys gradually forced the French troops back from the water's edge, but it was evident that, before Marlborough could launch his main effort against Tallard, he had to deal with the problem of Oberglau. The village, although smaller than Blindheim, had been strongly fortified by Marsin's infantry, who had taken care to break down the fences and hedges around the cottages, to improve fields of fire.

Oberglau sat squarely to the right flank of Churchill's infantry

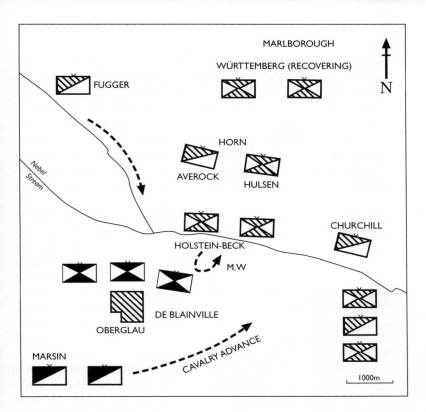

The Allied attack on Oberglau.

as they advanced from the line of the Nebel stream. The Prince of
Holstein-Beck (who had ridden to join the army only the previous
day) was directed by Count Horn to move forward with two
brigades of Dutch infantry and secure the village. As with the
Danish squadrons before them, they struggled through the mud
of the stream and were confronted by a stout line of French
infantry between the water and the cottages. The Dutch were
then struck by a smart counter-attack mounted by the red-coated
émigré Irish regiments in French service – Clare, Dorrington and
Lee. Such was the ferocity of the Irish attack that the two leading
Dutch battalions, those of Goor and Benheim, were routed and
dispersed. Holstein-Beck called for assistance to some Imperial
cavalry standing nearby, but their commander, Count Fugger,
refused to move without orders. Valiantly trying to rally his
soldiers the Prince was captured, and the Irish soldiers took him
away, mortally wounded, on a hand-cart.

   This was potentially a very serious development. For Marsin to complete the rout of Holstein-Beck's Dutch column would threaten to split the Allied army in two, and give the French and Bavarians the one real chance that day to defeat their opponents in detail. Eugene's smaller Wing would be isolated from that of Marlborough, and the initiative would pass to the French and Bavarians. A crisis was at hand, for the battle was at full-pitch across the wide plain. Merode-Westerloo wrote of the moment: 'From one end of the armies to the other every one was at grips and all fighting at once.' Marsin saw the chance to break Eugene and Marlborough apart, and ordered his cavalry to change front, from facing Eugene, towards their right and the open flank of Churchill's infantry, drawn up in front of Unterglau. The French squadrons, a little tired from their efforts that afternoon but still in good order, cantered forward past Oberglau and the Irish regiments, who opened ranks to allow them past. However, the haste of their advance, and the marshy ground underfoot, meant that the French commanders had to pause to realign their squadrons for a proper charge; this was without doubt necessary, but it gave Marlborough just enough time to receive them.

Prussian grenadier and infantryman, c.1704.

The Duke, seeing the savaging of Holstein-Beck's column by the Irish troops, had already crossed the Nebel on a makeshift bridge to get a closer view. He ordered Hulsen's brigade to move forward to the support of the Dutch, and these veteran German battalions,

Cutts's British infantry approach

French garrison in Blindheim

Tallard's cavalry

Marlborough's cavalry and infantry form up after crossing the Nebel stream.

Blindheim church tower seen from the plain of Höchstädt. The French and Allied cavalry struggled over these fields all the afternoon of 13 August 1704.

changing front to their right, moved quickly into place. A Dutch cavalry brigade under Averock was called forward and they were supported by another of Blood's batteries that the energetic colonel had dragged up to their aid: 'Nine field pieces loaded with partridge [canister] shot', as Captain Robert Parker remembered. Averock's squadrons were soon under pressure though and in danger of being overwhelmed by Marsin's more numerous cavalry. Marlborough now sent word to Fugger, standing with his Imperial Cuirassier brigade near to Weilheim Farm, with an appeal to help deflect Marsin's cavalry thrust. The Count, who had just refused to move to help Holstein-Beck, moved promptly forward on Marlborough's request. As a result, Marsin's troopers found that, as they moved forward against Churchill's flank, Fugger's squadrons threatened them on their left side, the bridle arm (the weaker side away from the sabre arm). The muddy mess of the Nebel stream lay between the opposing squadrons, but the French were forced to change front to meet the looming threat from the cuirassiers, and so the chance to strike with any force at Marlborough's infantry passed.

The Duke now directed Count Berensdorf, who took the command of the Dutch infantry as Holstein-Beck had fallen, to pen Marsin's French and Irish infantry in Oberglau, so that they could not again threaten Churchill's flank as he advanced against Tallard. With support from Blood's batteries the Dutch, Hessians and Hanoverian infantry fought a tough battle to drive the opposing troops back into the village. The fighting was prolonged, with costly close-quarter bayonet fighting, but eventually this was achieved. The Marquis de Blainville, the French commander in the village, was among those killed as he rallied the Poitou Régiment for the last of several desperate counter-charges that afternoon. The losses on both sides in the struggle for Oberglau village were severe and the Goor Regiment was entirely wrecked in the fighting with only fifty men left on their feet at the end of the battle (the most severe unit loss in the Allied army). The following day Marlborough offered sympathy to their distraught commander, saying that he wished he had stood in Colonel Goor's place. The Dutch officer tartly replied that he too wished it, as 'I should have had a good regiment, and you would have been without one.'

Meanwhile, at about 4pm Marlborough calmly sent an aide, Lord Tunbridge, with a message to Eugene, who was in the saddle and fighting hand-to-hand with Bavarian cavalry near to Lutzingen, that all was well on the left of the field. If the Prince would just keep Marsin and the Elector occupied, he would now destroy Tallard's cavalry. Eugene was perfectly prepared to do so, but he was exasperated at the failing energy of his own Imperial cavalry in the hacking, slashing fights along the stream. He had already threatened to shoot some troopers who hung back from the fray, and now went to fight with Anhalt-Dessau's infantry,

Marlborough forces Tallard back.

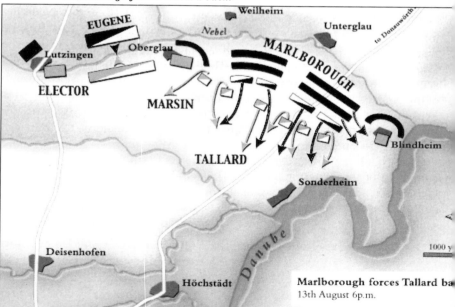

Marlborough forces Tallard ba
13th August 6p.m.

The Dead Man's Wage

This curious expression had two meanings during the War of the Spanish Succession. Firstly, it refers to the unofficial, but widespread practice of carrying a non-existent 'Dead Man' on the muster rolls of each company in a regiment. Pay was drawn for the 'Dead Man' and used for the relief of the widows and orphans of the regiment – the system of pensions at this time being imperfect to the extent that for most it did not exist at all. Although this system was sometimes open to abuse and embezzlement, the money raised in this practical way was highly appreciated. The system, although having no official standing, was recognised by Queen Anne, who took a great interest in the correct application of the funds raised. 'The Secretary at War requested [stated] that the pension fund was exhausted, but the Queen has directed that one man per troop should be mustered under a fictitious name, whereby the fund for the Flanders widows would be enlarged, and the pensions paid more regularly.'

The other use for the expression 'Dead Man's Wage' was in connection with the bounty money often offered to volunteers for a particularly hazardous task, such as the storming of a breach in fortress walls. The money would be pooled and paid out to the survivors of the action, who enjoyed not only their own bounty, but that of their fallen comrades. John Scot, who fought through all the Duke of Marlborough's campaigns, and took part in many such desperate actions, wrote that the survivors: 'Took the dead man's wage, and the price of their blood.'

muttering that he preferred to die among brave men: 'See, they don't retreat before the enemy although they are attacked with a three-fold superior force.' Eugene's weary cavalry were left in position facing the Elector's equally ragged squadrons across the Nebel. At Lutzingen the Prince's wish was soon almost granted, as a Bavarian trooper levelled his carbine at his head at close range. A Danish soldier stepped forward to spit the Bavarian with his bayonet before he could fire. The time was about 4.30pm, and the August sun shone on the striving soldiers across the breadth of the plain with unrelenting warmth.

Chapter 6

A GLORIOUS VICTORY

WITH CLERAMBAULT'S INFANTRY crammed into Blindheim village, unable mostly to manoeuvre or use their muskets to any effect, while Eugene pressed remorselessly forward against the Bavarian defenders of Lutzingen, the time had come for Marlborough to launch his assault on Tallard. The French and Walloon cavalry on the plain of Höchstädt were hot and weary after the scrambling, fruitless battles along the Nebel stream. They had few infantry supports, Clerambault had seen to that, but nine small battalions of young troops, the regiments of de Bellisle, de Beil and de Robecq, stood beside the Höchstädt road to offer what support they could. Tallard ordered three battalions forward to support more closely the first line squadrons, but nothing was done to help them, and they fell back before heavy fire from Blood's batteries, leaving a trail of broken men behind. Merode-Westerloo, who commanded the second line of the French right Wing cavalry that day, wrote of the imperfect ordering and slack handling of the French cavalry on this part of the field:

> *Our senior Generals had been pleased to leave too great an interval between our first and second lines. When the enemy attacked Blenheim in two-column strength, and the Gendarmerie charged... I wanted to advance with the second line [cavalry] to support them, but the French high command would not allow [it]. The broken, disordered cavalry poured through the intervals between my own squadrons; the Gendarmerie was undoubtedly soundly beaten, and the gallant Zurlauben received several grave wounds which caused his death two days later.*

Despite this the Comte led his second line squadrons to the charge:

> *I came face to face with the enemy after he passed the stream, and my fresh, well-ordered squadrons charged and flung them back, right over the Nebel; following them up, we then attacked their second line, which also crumbled; but then we came up against a third, untired force, and my squadrons,*

84

disordered and blown by their exertions, were themselves
defeated and pushed back over the stream.
According to Merode-Westerloo, the French squadrons on his left
gave ground too soon and allowed the Allied cavalry the chance
to gain the higher part of the plain:

They had given ground to the enemy, who were pouring over
the stream and forming up on my flank in the very midst of our
army, the centre of which was now under the command of the
Duc d'Humieres [after the wounding of von Zurlauben]
conspicuous in his fine gilt cuirass.

At just after 5pm Marlborough glanced to left and right – all was
ready along the Allied line of battle. The two lines of cavalry had
now moved to the front of the Duke's line of battle, with the two
supporting lines of infantry behind them. He waved his cavalry
commanders forward – Lumley on the left with the first line of
English and Scots horse, and Hompesch on the right with the
Dutch and German squadrons. Some 8,000 troopers rode forward
in impressively good order, going quite slowly to conserve their
horses' strength on the upward incline away from the Nebel
stream. Höchstädt village was ahead of them and the church
tower, now picturesquely struck by the evening sun, could be
dimly seen ahead through the smoke and dust of the battlefield.
Marlborough's chaplain, Dr Hare, who interestingly makes no
mention of the third line of cavalry referred to by the Comte,
wrote:

The Duke of Marlborough had got the whole of the left wing
of the allied army over the rivulet, and our Horse were drawn
up in two lines fronting that of the enemy; but they did not offer
to charge till General Churchill had ranged all the Foot also in
two lines behind the cavalry.

Tallard's squadrons were ragged and tired. The Allied cavalry,
however, were still in good order due to the valuable support of
their infantry, whose steady musketry volleys broke up the
French cavalry attacks with ruthless efficiency. Merode-
Westerloo again:

They had brought their infantry well forward and they killed
and wounded many of our horses. This was followed by an
authorised but definite movement to the rear by my men – and
I too, would have been obliged to accompany them had not two
musket balls killed my horse beneath me, so that he subsided
gently to the ground... Luckily, however, one of my aides-de-

camp and a groom came up with yet another horse after observing my fall and they soon had me hoisted onto horseback again. I then reformed some sort of a line, and placed four pieces of artillery in front of my position – I had noticed them trying to sneak off.

The Comte then rode over to Blindheim and ordered the St Second and Montfort Régiments out from the constricted alleyways and into the open, to support his squadrons. For this presumption he was roundly abused by Clerambault, who ordered the infantrymen back into place, and Merode-Westerloo had to withdraw with as much grace as he could muster. His fresh horse was killed shortly afterwards, but his groom soon had him remounted.

The weary French cavalry pushed the first line Allied squadrons back on their infantry supports once again. Nerves were stretched on both sides, and the battle was not yet won. Marlborough at this time had to gently direct one of his cavalry officers not to take his squadrons off the field in the face of the French resistance: 'Sir, you are under a mistake, the enemy lies that way, you have nothing to do but to face them.' Now, at the Duke's command, the Allied second-line cavalry under von Bulow and the Count of Ost-Friese went forward at a trot. The French, tired and dispirited, could not resist the approaching wave of fresh troopers. Robert Parker remembered that: 'Our squadrons drove through the very centre of them, which put them to entire rout.' Suddenly, their composure broke, panic gripped the troopers, shouted commands were ignored, and entire squadrons had suddenly faced about and were galloping madly to the westwards, everyone attempting to escape the solid mass of Allied troopers who followed close behind.

With their cavalry in headlong flight, the French infantry were abandoned on the open plain. These nine battalions had not been drawn into Blindheim, but had faithfully maintained their position beside the Höchstädt road, giving quite effective support to Tallard's cavalry. Now those squadrons had fled, and the young soldiers had to face the full storm of Marlborough's army: horse, foot and guns brought forward to destroy them. Forming square against the Allied cavalry, the French infantrymen fought with desperate valour. Orkney afterwards wrote in admiration of their courage: 'They stood in battalion square in the best order I ever saw, until at last they were all cut down in rank and file.' Merode-

Marlborough engaged in a cavalry battle, c.1704.

Westerloo said of their plight:

> *The enemy had cut to ribbons seven* [sic] *newly raised French battalions after their easy deployment over the marshes. These unfortunate battalions had found themselves completely isolated in the centre, and died to a man where they stood, stationed right out in the open plain – supported by nobody.*

Meanwhile, the press of fugitive French cavalry was so great, that Merode-Westerloo's horse was borne up by others crowding in on either side, so that the hooves did not touch the ground for several hundred yards. The mass of horses and riders then tumbled down a bank near to the Danube, and the unhappy Comte was trampled and bruised before escaping with his dignity considerably battered. Helped to his feet by his head groom, Merode-Westerloo was back in the saddle, but the groom, Le Franc, was then shot and killed by an Allied cavalryman nearby. Meanwhile, numbers of the fleeing cavalry attempted to escape by swimming their horses across the river, but most who tried this desperate route drowned in the fast-flowing waters. The Duke of Marlborough's comment on this tragedy ran:

> *We cut off great numbers of them, as well in the action as in the retreat, besides upwards of 30 squadrons of the French, which we pushed into the Danube, where we saw the greatest part of them perish.*

The Allied pursuit.

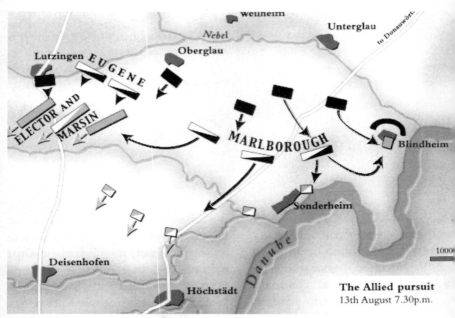

The Allied pursuit
13th August 7.30p.m.

The Allied cavalry charge at Blenheim, 1704, by H. Dupray.

The Marquis de Gruignan attempted a counter-attack with some companies of the Gens d'Armes, but this was brushed aside by the triumphant Allied cavalry. Tallard was nearby with small party of aides and he attempted without success to rally some of the broken squadrons about him. His shouted entreaties to stand and fight were not heard by the fleeing troopers, but he sent the Marquis de Maisonelle towards Blindheim to try and draw out some of Clerambault's infantry and make a stand in the open. This was all far too late to be effective, even if it could be done, and in any case, the Marquis was never seen again, and was presumably killed on the way.

A little later, as Tallard tried to escape from the field, he was confronted on a track near Sondersheim by a Hessian trooper from Bothmar's dragoons and taken prisoner. The Marshal was conducted to the Prince of Hesse-Cassell, and was sent on under escort to Marlborough, who was near the Höchstädt road with his

The destruction of the French infantry on the plain of Höchstädt.

cavalry commanders, watching the pursuit of the broken French army. With elaborate courtesy the Duke welcomed Tallard: 'I am very sorry that such a cruel misfortune should have fallen upon a soldier for whom I have the highest regard'. The Marshal murmured in reply: 'And I congratulate you on defeating the best soldiers in the world'. With crushing civility Marlborough replied, 'Your Lordship, I presume, excepts those who had the honour to beat them?' The Marshal was then put into Marlborough's own coach and provided with refreshment. He was soon joined by several other of his senior officers as the scooping up of prisoners went on through the evening. The day was doubly tragic for Tallard, as he had seen his own young son killed in the action earlier that afternoon.

While Tallard's army was on the rack, the Danish and Prussian infantry under Anhalt-Dessau pressed forward once again in a third desperate attack on the Bavarian strongpoint of Lutzingen. Just two stalwart squadrons of Imperial cavalry shielded their left flank. Prince Eugene went into the attack with them, while the Dessauer fought on foot, waving a regimental colour over his head to encourage his infantrymen onwards. As before the Bavarian artillery was brutally efficient, with canister and round-shot tearing the ranks of the attacking infantry, but the Prussians disregarded their losses and stormed into the great battery. They were in no mood for prisoners, and the gun crews fought with a frenzy for the possession of the pieces, and were cut down without mercy. Beyond the village Scholten's Danes drove the French infantry for over a mile through the copses in a bitterly fought hand-to-hand bayonet struggle, which left the groves thickly scattered with broken bodies in their blue, grey and white uniforms.

Despite the cost of their assault, the Allied infantry had now unhinged the left flank of the whole French and Bavarian line, and with Tallard in full flight on the far side of the plain, it was clear that Marsin and the Elector had to go or risk annihilation. Merode-Westerloo, never slow to stress his own contribution to events, wrote that:

> *They ordered a retreat, which was carried out in good order; but I believe they would not have escaped so easily but for my men keeping the enemy's attention fully occupied. Otherwise the foe could have attacked the head and flank of our left Wing as it retreated towards Lavingen. As things turned out, however, our entire left got safely away.*

The position that had been occupied by Marsin was strong and his flanks were secured by his colleagues, at least until Tallard's army fled. His army was numerically stronger than that of Eugene, and able to deploy at least as many guns as the Prince could drag into action. Marsin had nonetheless allowed himself to be fixed in position by the persistent attacks that came in across the fields from Schwennenbach and Weilheim Farm, even though the energy of the Imperial troops faltered as the afternoon and evening wore on. The Marshal, a virulent critic of the shortcomings of others, had both failed to deal with Eugene effectively, or to support fully either Tallard on his right or the Elector to his left. Even Oberglau, strongly held by French and Irish infantry, he had allowed to be blockaded, so that Churchill's

The surrender of Tallard to Bothmar's dragoons, by R. Caton Woodville.

infantry could pass it by without interference to his right flank as he advanced. Marsin did successfully get his troops off the battlefield, but they should have been called on to do more that day.

Tallard's army had broken and run away, and the French and Bavarians of the left Wing were now moving in full, if well ordered, retreat towards the hamlets of Diesenhofen and Morselingen. Any delay might mean a running fight to pass the gap between the hills and the Danube, and Marlborough ordered Hompesch to press the retreating enemy with his cavalry. These Dutch and German squadrons had fought hard and were tired, and in the failing light they mistook some of Eugene's Imperial cavalry, just then moving forward past Oberglau, for the French. Robert Parker wrote of the incident:

Prince Eugene by this time had a good part of his troops over the morass [Nebel stream], *and was just ready to fall on their rear; but perceiving the squadrons under Hompesch coming down that way, he took them to be some of Tallard's squadrons drawing down to join the Elector; whereby he halted, lest they should fall on his flank. The Duke also seeing Prince Eugene's troops so near the rear of the Elector's army, took them to be a body of Bavarians, making good the Elector's retreat; and there-upon ordered Hompesch to halt. Here they remained until they were informed of their mistakes by their Aides de Camp, and it was by this means that the Elector and Marsin had time to get over the pass. Our troops also were much fatigued, and night drew on.*

The Allied troopers had halted and by the time the confusion was sorted out, Marsin and the Elector had opened a gap with their pursuers, achieving something close to a clean break as they withdrew westwards. Nearby, Merode-Westerloo, although bruised after his adventures at the river's edge, was sufficiently recovered to try and rally the surviving French troops of the right Wing:

I went into the square [of Höchstädt] *where I found several French generals who had the nerve to tell me that I was pretty late. I retorted that they, for their part, had arrived too soon. We then all had a drink at the fountain... I passed through the little town and came out on the ridge beyond the marsh* [the wet ground where Tallard had decided not to place his camp], *and there I found all the debris of our cavalry in*

Prussian dragoon c.1704.

indescribable confusion. It was almost eight o'clock when I reached them; I at once settled down to work, as nobody else was doing anything about the disorder. First I posted a troop of twenty or thirty Gendarmerie on the road which I had followed to Hochstadt; it was only a narrow lane, but it offered the enemy the only approach to the town. One hundred yards back I drew up a second troop, and then another and another so on all along the ridge... Fugitives at last began to look for their units.

Despite the Comte's praiseworthy efforts, there was no disguising the fact that Tallard's cavalry was shattered both physically and morally as a fighting unit. The best that could be hoped for was that those that could still ride would get away to safety.

Meanwhile, the French infantry clung tenaciously to their hold on Blindheim village. With such numbers of troops crammed into the narrow streets, many of the French soldiers had no field of fire, and the Allied soldiers increasingly pressed through the gardens and orchards around the village to sweep the narrow exits with ruthlessly efficient musketry. As the day progressed Allied batteries were increasingly brought into position to batter the village and its defenders. Despite their relative inactivity the French infantry suffered casualties in significant numbers, and the wounded and maimed were thrust into the cottages for shelter. The Régiment du Roi, in particular, initially deployed at the edge of the small Maulweyer stream, which runs into Blindheim from the plain, had losses from artillery fire directed at breaking up the ranks of the Gens d'Armes who stood nearby.

Still, the British and German brigades had insufficient strength to force their way past the barricades, and Marlborough had to turn away from the pursuit of his broken opponents to direct Churchill to detach more infantry and storm the village. This diversion may have hindered the pursuit of the French squadrons, but the French panic lent speed to their horses

94

hooves, and there was not a lot the Allied foot soldiers could do now to catch them. Earl Orkney's infantry, Hamilton's British brigade and St Paul's Hanoverians moved across the trampled wheat towards the cottages. Under this pressure the French gradually fell back towards the centre of the place, where a bitter struggle with bayonet and musket butt continued around the walled churchyard, which had been prepared for defence. Soon Churchill had to send in the dismounted dragoons of Hay and Ross to add weight to Orkney's attack, but progress, where it was gained at all, was hard won.

Colonel Belville's Hanoverian Zell battalions, leaving the scene of the destruction of the young French infantry, were also fed into the brawling battle. The Hanoverians steadied the resolve of Hay's and Ross's dragoons, who were recoiling from a smart French counter-charge delivered by the regiments of Artois and Provence, under command of Colonel de la Silvière. Tramping across the muddy Maulweyer stream, the rallied troops went into the attack once more, and the defenders were driven back at bayonet point through the smoking alleys towards the church-yard. Progress was painfully slow for the French infantry fought with their customary courage and, despite appalling casualties, they refused to be driven. With so much debris lying in the streets, only a few men could advance at a time and the French took a terrible toll on the attackers, as the blood price for the ground that the Allied soldiers gained. Many of the cottages were now burning – the repeated discharges of muskets and the Allied artillery fire saw to that. Also, Orkney wrote that some cottages were deliberately set alight, so that the

George Hamilton, 1st Earl Orkney (1666–1737), by Maingaud. He commanded British infantry at Blenheim.

95

The British dragoons assault Blindheim village, evening 13 August 1704, by R. Caton Woodville.

French field of fire should be obscured by the smoke, and the defenders driven out by the flames. The wounded, who had hoped to find shelter, were burning to death and their terrible screams added to the mayhem of that ghastly evening. John Deane still stood wearily at the edge of the village nearest the stream, and wrote later:

Many on both sides were burnt to death. Great and grevious were the cryes of the maimed, and those suffering in the flames.

At this time Tallard, hearing the persistent roar of musketry from the village, sent a message to Marlborough, offering to send an order to the garrison to withdraw from the field. The Duke was in the saddle near Morselingen, conferring with Hompesch on another attempt to disrupt Marsin's withdrawal. He was visibly irritated by what he saw as the captive Marshal's presumption, and his cool reply was: 'Inform M. Tallard that, in the position in which he now is, he has no command.'

Nonetheless, as dusk came on Marlborough was anxious for the outcome in the village. The French garrison, infantry and dragoons, had been abandoned in the chaos that enveloped Tallard. Clerambault was nowhere to be found, and his aide afterwards told how he had drowned in a vain effort to swim his horse across the Danube. A crisis of command in the village was evident. The Marquis de Denonville had been wounded in the thigh with a bayonet thrust and he and the Régiment du Roi were virtually cut off in the part of Blindheim that they held, having thrown Orkney's infantry back no fewer than three times. Now the Earl tried another way: 'It came into my head to beat a parley' he wrote afterwards to a friend. Denonville agreed to a temporary cease-fire where his regiment stood, to allow the wounded to be dragged out of burning cottages. In the pause in the firing this brought about, Colonel Belville was sent forward with Denonville by beat of drum to parley with the Marquis de Blanzac who, in Clerambault's absence, took on the burden of this doomed command. The Marquis was conducted to where Orkney stood with his grimy soldiers at the barricades. The Earl, although aware of his lack of numbers in the face of the powerful garrison, behaved with great coolness and pressed de Blanzac on the futility of continued resistance. Surely, he urged the Frenchman, to fight on would be to needlessly sacrifice the lives of his faithful infantry. The Marquis, of course, was not aware of Orkney's

Marlborough writing the Blenheim Despatch, 13 August 1704, by R. Hillingford. Courtesy Dr David Chandler.

numerical weakness and was reluctantly persuaded of the need to capitulate. As darkness fell, nearly 10,000 of France's best infantry laid down their arms and surrendered their colours.

One of Orkney's young aides, James Abercrombie, impetuously spurred his horse forward and attempted to seize the regimental colour of the Régiment du Roi. 'I rode up to the Royal regiment and pulled the colours out of the Ensign's hands.' Affronted at the insult, the French ensign struck Abercrombie a glancing blow with his sword across the outstretched forearm. The young aide had to withdraw with what good grace he could muster, and wait for the formal surrender of the treasured symbol. As it was, the Navarre Régiment, in the bitterness of their disgrace, burned their colours rather than hand them over – a pointless gesture, as they surrendered themselves anyway. The French capitulation came not a moment too soon for, at this late point

Ensign, French regiment, c.1700.

in the evening, the battle seemed far from won. Abercrombie wrote that:

> My Lord Duke's Aide de Camp came and acquainted My Lord [Orkney] that his Grace had sent him to inform Him that he should lie upon his Arms that Night and that he would join Him next morning with All the Foot and Cannon He could get and Attack the Village.

During these exciting events, Marlborough was still in the saddle and conducting a weary pursuit of the broken remnants of the French and Bavarians. Pausing in the operation, he borrowed an old tavern bill from an aide and, dismounting, scribbled a brief note on the back in pencil. He handed this makeshift despatch to Colonel Daniel Parke, a rakish Virginia-born volunteer, to take to Duchess Sarah in London:

> I have not time to say more but to beg you will give my duty to the Queen and let her know that her Army has had a glorious victory. M. Tallard and two other generals are in my coach and I am following the rest. The bearer, Colonel Parke, will give her an account of what has passed. I shall doe it in a day or two by another more at large.

Parke flogged his horses along and, eight days later, that same scrappy note was handed to Queen Anne in the long gallery in Windsor Castle. The Queen in this way learned that, at her wish, the Captain-General had destroyed one of France's main field armies in open battle, and that Louis XIV's war plans lay in ruins. In Versailles, meanwhile, a grand masque to celebrate the triumph of the River Seine over all rivers of Europe was enjoyed by the court. Smiles were strained, however, for rumours abounded that a reverse had been suffered in the Danube valley. French officers, now in Allied hands, were writing home setting their affairs in order. When the dreadful news arrived, no one could

Colonel Daniel Parke, c.1704. He took the Blenheim Despatch to London.

99

Marlborough hands the Blenheim Despatch to Parke.

QR   Augest 13 '1904

I have not time to say more, but to beg you will give my Duty to the Queen, and Let her know Her Army has had a Glorious Victory Mons.^sr Tallard and two other Generals are in my Coach and I am following the rest the bearer my Aide Camp C: M Parker will give Her and account of what has pass'd, I shall do it in a day or two at another more at large

Marlboroug

Marlborough's handwritten despatch to inform Queen Anne of his victory at Blenheim.

credit the scale of the defeat for French arms, and Louis XIV was so stunned by the news that it was thought at first that he had suffered a stroke. The Duc de St Simon wrote: 'One was not accustomed to misfortune...what was the anguish of the King.' In Vienna, by contrast, the Emperor declared three days of rejoicing at the victory.

For much of the day the armies had been in close and deadly conflict. According to John Deane:

> As for those killed upon the spot I believe few or none can pretend to give that account being a thing seeming almost impossible; butt this I can and will affirm that the earth was covered in a manner for English miles together wth dead bodys of both armies soe that from any more such sights good God deliver me. The battle being over; and the field our own, we lay upon our armes that night.

In the darkness of the night of battle, the Allied infantry, Deane wrote, 'Formed a lane wherein the prisoners stood all night.' The Duke slept for three hours in a mill on the edge of Höchstädt that had been used by the French to store gunpowder, but no misfortune happened to disturb his rest.

Somewhere to the west, the Comte de Merode-Westerloo, after a hectic day, was able to relax a little:

> After being in the saddle for thirty hours with neither sleep nor food and only one drink of water. My knee was swollen to the size of a man's head; although a bullet had been fired at me at point blank range, it had failed to penetrate thanks to my strong thigh boots with thick flaps down to the knees; beneath these I had worn a pair of stockings to keep off the flies, and my underwear. The bullet had got as far as my stocking, but had penetrated no farther.

At the roadside, somewhere west of Morselingen, the Elector of Bavaria was writing to his wife with news of the disaster to their family fortunes. They had, he wrote, lost everything that day: 'Wir haben heute alles verloren'. Louis XIV's scheming ally was now a fugitive.

The cost of the battle was extraordinary and added to the wonder with which the world greeted the news of Marlborough's victory. The scale of the victors' casualties illustrates the vigour with which the French and Bavarians fought them that day. Over 9,000 men from Marlborough's Wing were killed or wounded, and nearly 5,000 from Eugene's smaller Wing. Of these the valiant

at Alvost Camp. 1707,
ch Execution of Deserters in Flanders 1707

Execution of deserters, c.1707.

Danish infantry suffered a stunning 2,401 casualties (1,355 of them killed) in their bitter fight with de Rozel's French for possession of the woods beyond Lutzingen, while the British toll on the left flank was 2,234 killed and wounded. On the other side of the hill, the loss to the French and Bavarian army was simply staggering. Some 20,000 soldiers were killed and wounded, and an amazing 14,000 unharmed prisoners fell into Allied hands (of whom 12,149 were French). No less than forty of those taken prisoner were general officers, who tamely surrendered themselves so dazed were they by the day's awful events. Two veteran units in French service, the Walloon Zurlauben Régiment and the German Gueder Régiment, volunteered for Allied service rather then face the rigours of being Imperial prisoners of war. The Allied booty included over 100 guns and mortars, 129 infantry colours and 110 cavalry standards, 5,400 wagons and coaches (some containing rather exotically dressed officers' 'ladies'), 7,000 horses and mules and 3,600 tents. So great was the haul that much of the huge pile of camp stores, forage, food, ammunition, harness and campaign gear that was seized by the Allies could never be counted, and was unavoidably abandoned on the plain of Höchstädt to be pillaged or to rot.

The morning after the battle, Marlborough visited Tallard and his senior officers, all captive at the quarters of the Prince of Hesse-Cassell. The Marshal had suffered a slight wound to his hand the previous day, which was being dressed, and he asked that his carriage should be obtained. The Duke

The Elector of Bavaria, Louis XIV's scheming ally.

sent a messenger after the retreating French and Bavarian armies, to ask that Tallard's equipage should be sent back to the Allied army, for the captive Marshal's convenience.

Despite the magnificence of their victory, the Allied army had experienced a very severe test that day, and Eugene wrote that: 'I have not a squadron or a battalion which did not charge four times at least.' In truth, one army broke and ran, but only after a hard fight. Once the victorious army had gathered itself, and a distribution of prisoners and booty was arranged between Marlborough and Eugene, the pursuit could begin in earnest. Some Allied regiments, however, were so shattered that they were beyond campaigning without full reconstitution and filling of ranks with recruits. Many of the battalions in Marlborough's Wing of the army, in particular, had suffered heavily at the Schellenberg fight, and had received no battlefield casualty replacements since. Their ranks were even thinner after the heavy fighting on the plain of Höchstädt. Not surprisingly, a certain weariness overcame them all, high and low, as the troops paused to savour their immense achievement.

Not the least of the difficulties was what to do with the vast haul of prisoners. Marlborough wrote to London four days after the battle:

> *The number of prisoners increases hourly, for the soldiers*

103

Camille d'Hostun, Duc de Tallard

Tallard was granted a commission in the French army at the age of fifteen; by the time he was forty-one he was a Lieutenant-General, and was made Marshal in 1702 after the victory at Speyerbach. Tallard was conscientious, and did not lack bravery, but his friendship with King Louis XIV sustained him in a position of high rank which his otherwise limited abilities perhaps did not merit. However, his calm influence as French Ambassador in London had been of great use both to William III and Louis XIV, and his expulsion in 1702 was an error. His bold operations to march through the Black Forest and support Marsin's army in Bavaria, twice during 1704, were well handled on the whole, and a great credit to the Marshal.

A commander with more grip would not have permitted the Marquis de Clerambault to shut most of the infantry of the French right Wing into Blindheim village. He was physically short-sighted, which may have hampered him in the smoke and dust of a battlefield. Taken as a prisoner back to England by Marlborough, Tallard was kept in comfortable confinement in Nottingham, where his charm and good manners soon endeared him to the local gentry. The Marshal was disappointed by the food provided, and taught his gaolers to make French bread. He also found celery growing wild, and introduced it to the locals as a delicacy hitherto

Camille d'Hostun, Duc de Tallard, Marshal of France (1652–1728).

unknown in England.

On the signing of the Treaty of Utrecht in 1713, Tallard was released and returned to France. Nearly ten years had elapsed since the great disaster to French arms over which he had presided, and no one could foresee the kind of reception he would receive in Versailles. However, Louis XIV appeared to bear the broken Marshal no ill will. As the elderly man stooped to kneel, the King took a step forward to receive him, a shocking and unprecedented gesture by the proud monarch. Lifting Tallard gently to his feet, the King murmured 'Welcome back, old friend.'

*that in the rout dispersed themselves into the country, finding
no safety there, come and surrender themselves. The Marshal*
[Tallard] *with some of the chief officers, will be going on
Tuesday* [22 August] *to Franckfort and Hanau. I shall send a
captain with forty or fifty English horse for their guard, and we
shall endeavour to dispose of the rest in the best manner as
soon as possible, for they are not only very troublesome, but
oblige us to remain here while we should be pursuing our blow
and following the enemy.*

Meanwhile, the Comte de Merode-Westerloo, after refreshing
himself for a few days in Ulm, wrote that:

*When we learnt that the enemy was on the march after
capture of Ingolstadt we left the neighbourhood of Ulm. If the
foe had been quick enough, not one of us would have escaped.
I should have mentioned that the moment we left Ulm all the
heavy baggage and carts were set on fire in the interests of
mobility.*

The Comte's comments may be viewed in light of the admirable
turn of speed with which he and his comrades left the field of
battle. Certainly, the exertions of the Allied troops were such that
the pursuit of the beaten enemy was less active than might
otherwise be expected. The sorry remnants of Tallard's army,
and the still intact, more or less, forces of Marsin and the Elector
were able to draw off without too close a harrying. Their morale
was broken of course, and desertions from the Bavarian ranks
were numerous – the French were less inclined to desert as the
local peasants would (as Marlborough hinted at in his letter) be
likely to lynch any they laid hands on.

All Bavaria was now under the control of the Allies, and the
Elector was a fugitive, taking the remnants of his army to the
Spanish Netherlands, where he was still the Governor-General,
courtesy of Louis XIV. Marlborough pursued Marsin back to the
frontiers of France, as far as the exhaustion of his army permitted.
Plans for an autumn campaign in the Moselle valley, however, did
not progress very well. The French recovered their poise and the
Duke's subordinates fumbled their operations. The onset of cold
weather saw the Allied army having to pull back to Coblenz, and
the troops went off to winter quarters. Marlborough then went to
London to receive his Triumph. He landed at Greenwich on 14
December 1704 along with Marshal Tallard and thirty-five of the
more senior officers taken prisoner in the great battle. The

The north face of Blenheim Palace, c.1745. By kind permission of His Grace the Duke of Marlborough.

cavalry standards and regimental colours from Tallard's shattered army were taken in solemn procession to Westminster Hall. Later they were put in St Paul's Cathedral where they rotted away so that within 135 years there was nothing left of them to be seen.

The Duke of Marlborough received a solemn address from the House of Lords, which gives a flavour of the sensation felt throughout Britain at the scale of the victory at Blenheim:

> *The happy success that has attended Her Majesty's arms under Your Grace's conduct in Germany in the last campaign, so truly great, so truly glorious in all its circumstances, that*

Medal struck to commemorate the victory of Marlborough and Eugene.

few instances in former ages equal, much less excel the lustre of it. Your Grace has not over thrown young and unskilful generals, raw and undisciplined troops, but Your Grace has conquered the French and Bavarian armies, that were fully instructed in the arts of war; select veteran troops, flushed with former successes and victories, commanded by generals of great experience and bravery.

Among the many rewards that came to the Duke of Marlborough after the victory, Queen Anne gifted her triumphant general the royal hunting estate at Woodstock in Oxfordshire, together with funds to build a great palace there. The erection of the building, known as Blenheim Palace, took many years and became the subject of some controversy as the Duke's influence at court eventually waned. The palace is the home of the Dukes of Marlborough to the present day, and the quit rent paid every year to the sovereign is the standard of the French Régiment du Roi, which surrendered to Marlborough's troops in Blindheim village that summer day in 1704.

Chapter 7

THE ARMIES AT BLENHEIM

HE DUKE OF MARLBOROUGH commanded a confederate army at Blenheim, with the combined forces of Britain, Holland and Imperial Austria delivering a stunning blow to French military power and prestige. The troops who marched southwards with the Duke from the Low Countries that fateful summer were almost all in English pay, but they were not only drawn from Queen Anne's regiments, for many Protestant German states (Hesse, Hanover, Zell, Brandenburg/Prussia) all contributed excellent troops, as did Denmark. These were provided by their princes in return for English gold and, in a strict sense, were mercenary troops. However, they were almost uniformly of excellent quality and firm loyalty, and their professional prowess and ability to take heavy losses without flinching was widely acknowledged. Johan Goor's Dutch corps, which had been operating on the Upper Rhine frontier with the Margrave of Baden, was put under the Duke's command as the great march progressed, and these troops comprised both Dutch and Protestant Swiss and German troops in the pay of the States-General. Again, the quality was high and their achievements on the field of battle considerable.

Prince Eugene, in theory at least, was of equal rank with Marlborough – he was certainly the senior field commander for Austria in the Danube campaign (a fact that galled the Margrave of Baden considerably). Marlborough and Eugene struck up an immediate accord and, aware of the sensitivities of coalition warfare, they co-operated together very closely throughout the entire campaign. This relationship was of enormous value to their operations, and there was no jealously or suspicion to cloud their views as they worked together. However, Eugene deferred to Marlborough as the representative of Queen Anne, and the commander in the field of the Anglo-Dutch forces. The Prince had the wisdom to see that Austria depended upon her allies at this stage of the war to a far greater degree than they depended upon her. Marlborough's own good sense and good manners ensured that he treated the Prince with the utmost respect, and the troops

Prince Eugene of Savoy. His sacrificial attacks pinned down the French and Bavarian left Wing.

understood this, so no unhealthy rivalry sprang up to hamper their efforts.

The Austrian army comprised large numbers of 'German' Imperial troops – from Swabia, Württemberg, Baden, Anhalt and Mecklenberg. While their standard of training and equipment may not quite have matched that of the Anglo-Dutch forces, their courage was not in doubt, despite Eugene's exasperation with his cavalry at a certain lack of fire at one stage of the assault on Lutzingen.

On the other side of the hill, the French and Bavarian army presented an equally mixed picture, although, as with their opponents, the soldiers themselves were both brave and proficient in the use of their arms. The Elector of Bavaria's army was tough and well trained, but it was small in number. This lack

Officer's spontoon, c.1700.

was made dramatically worse by the destruction of D'Arco's corps at the Schellenberg, for the Count had been given the best available troops to hold this important point, and their almost complete loss was a sore blow to the Elector. The Allied campaign of destruction in Bavaria that followed the battle at Donauwörth made things worse, for the Elector felt obliged to send detachments of troops to dispersed points to protect his own estates. Ironically enough, Marlborough had given orders that the Elector's estates were not to be ravaged, not so much out of a quaint sense of chivalry, but more to antagonise the Bavarian people who saw their own barns and farms go up in flames while their ruler's possessions remained intact. The French bitterly complained at the dispersal of the Bavarian troops on these tactically unproductive tasks but the Elector refused to heed them. The effect was that, on the day of battle at Blenheim, most of the Bavarian army was absent, and only five battalions of infantry were available to fight alongside their French allies.

The French army of Marshal Marsin had been on campaign in Bavaria for some time, and was generally composed of fit, well-trained veteran troops. Marsin may have lacked the long experience of other Marshals (being the youngest of their number), but he was an able and darkly ruthless commander, ambitious and well used to getting the best out of his soldiers. The army that Marshal Tallard led from the Rhine to the Danube was, by contrast, of rather mixed quality. The Swiss infantry in Louis XIV's service declined to cross the Rhine, and their place in the French order of battle was taken by the young and inexperienced regiments that suffered in the slaughter of the closing moments of the battle of the plain of Höchstädt. Their bravery was evident in the sacrifice they made on the day, but the soldiers had not been given the time and experience to become first-rate campaigners. Also, the constant demands on Louis XIV from courtiers anxious to secure prestigious commands in the French army for relatives and friends, induced the King to constantly raise new regiments, to satisfy the demand for posts, rather than to send new recruits to replace battle losses in existing veteran regiments. This led to a gradual wasting of the experienced regiments, while raw troops took their place in the line of battle alongside the veterans.

The cavalry that Tallard brought to the Danube was also of varied quality. There were many elite units such as the Gendarmerie and the excellent Walloon regiments of Heider, Caetano and Acosta, but the rigours of the awful march through the Black Forest, which had worn out the mounts, had been made worse by an epidemic of glanders. This sickness caused the loss of about one-third of Tallard's cavalry horses during the march. There was no remount system in place for the French in Bavaria, and in any case time did not allow for the cavalry of the French right Wing to be brought up to full fettle before going into battle. The result was that Tallard's cavalry, the focal point for Marlborough's attack, was not in best condition to withstand the onslaught, even before their supporting infantry was snatched away into Blindheim village by Clerambault.

The Horse

At this time the cavalry (Horse) was still the battle-winning arm, although its power to dictate events in combat, evident under commanders such as Cromwell and Turenne in the previous century, was fast diminishing in the face of improved infantry weaponry and tactics. The speed and power of mounted troops had long proved effective on the battlefield using mobility and shock action to overwhelm the supposedly lesser mortals who fought on foot. The prime weapon of the cavalry was the sword (or sabre), as the use of the lance had not yet been revived in western Europe. The use of cold steel had evolved over the thirty years or so prior to Blenheim as a more effective tool than the rather feeble firearms that could be carried by a rider – the pistol, carbine and musketoon (a short musket with a blunderbuss type muzzle). Shock action was the key to success, driving an enemy in hopeless flight before your own massed squadrons. Some armies did cling to the outmoded use of firearms by their mounted troops, as with the Gendarmerie halting to fire their carbines at Palmes's British cavalry at Blenheim. This disrupted the onward progress of the French squadrons and enfeebled the shock action effect so much sought after by commanders. Marlborough's squadrons were not used in this hesitant way and 'Again and again in the course of the war the French squadrons were seen firing from the saddle with little or no effect, and the British crashing boldly into them and sweeping them away.' To ensure the Duke's troopers avoided bad habits, the Allied cavalry were only issued with three rounds each, for their pistols and carbines, to use when on picquet duty or foraging.

Cavalry in the armies on both sides were organised into squadrons, each usually comprising two troops. Each troop would muster, in the British army, some 62 men, and six troops would make up a regiment. The squadron was a tactical grouping of troops, varying according to circumstances, and a British cavalry regiment with six troops would, at full strength, put into the field 396 men including their twenty-six officers. Such a full muster would rarely be achieved outside peacetime, of course. The numbers in the other armies were broadly comparable, although the French squadrons were rather smaller. The squadrons would often be used on detached duty, so the six troops, or three squadrons, of a regiment charging together was quite unusual, and the cavalry brigades would often be made up of a mixture of those various squadrons available for use on the day.

Cavalry were costly to equip, mount, train and feed. Troopers were paid significantly more than foot soldiers (in recognition of their additional skill in the saddle). Good horsemen were not easy to obtain, so their tactical employment where heavy losses were likely called for the most careful thought. The gravity of the utter destruction of virtually all Tallard's cavalry at Blenheim may be viewed in light of this – those squadrons would not be easily replaced.

Given the expense of the cavalry, for all their glorious appearance, the tactical use of dragoons was increasing. These soldiers were basically mounted infantry, and they had a useful dual role. They were mustered in troops similar to the Horse, but their mounts were smaller than those of the cavalry, and therefore cheaper to obtain. The dragoons were equipped very much as the infantry (the Foot), often wearing stout shoes rather than boots. Their employment was largely in scouting, outpost work and, when dismounted, as infantry in either assault or defence. The added mobility their horses gave them was an important benefit, and they had the great advantage of being less expensive to employ than cavalry. With the growing demands of battle forcing commanders to deploy more and more horsemen to achieve the shock action so ardently desired, dragoons were increasingly used as pure cavalry, and their status and rates of pay would rapidly improve over time as a result.

The Foot

Traditionally considered to be a more humble breed than the cavalry, the infantry (the Foot) soldiers of an army were, in 1704 as now, the only combat arm capable of taking and holding ground. They were therefore the 'queen of the battlefield', the

Basic musketry drill, c.1700. Soldiers were taught to concentrate on the enemy's officers, colour bearers and drummers.

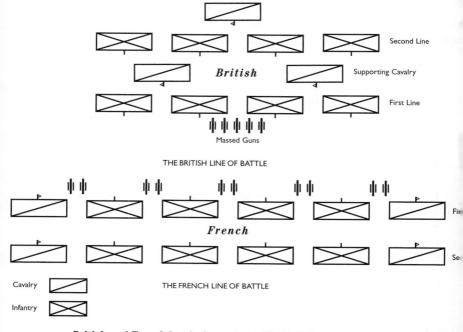

Cavalry Reserve

Second Line

British

Supporting Cavalry

First Line

Massed Guns

THE BRITISH LINE OF BATTLE

French

THE FRENCH LINE OF BATTLE

Cavalry

Infantry

British and French battle formations. The British interspersed their lines of cavalry and infantry, for mutual support. The French, fearing that the infantry would get in the way of the cavalry, did not do so.

bedrock on which all else rests, and infantry tactics had developed rapidly during the later half of the seventeenth century. The distinctive and differing employment of the pikeman and the musketeer had gone, as the almost universal introduction of the bayonet by the turn of the seventeenth century had finally made the long pike redundant (although its use lingered on in several armies, and reactionary generals never ceased, rather optimistically, to look for ways to employ the weapon again). Hitherto the foot soldier had been very vulnerable to attack by massed cavalry, particularly so since the demise of the longbow as a mainstream weapon some 150 years or more earlier. The slow firing and unreliable matchlock gave no real answer to the cavalry charge, even when closely supported by massed hedges of pikes. The development of the socket bayonet at this time, a less clumsy device than the earlier push-in 'plug' bayonet, enabled the foot soldier to load and fire his weapon while having the ability to use cold steel as necessary. The simple method was a significant advance in fighting technology, and enhanced the effectiveness of

114

Left: English pattern musket, c.1704. The work horse of the British infantry, it fired a heavier ball than its French counterpart.

Right: French musket, c.1704. It was better made than its English counterpart, but fired a lighter and less effective ball. (Not to scale)

infantry when faced with cavalry. The socket bayonet added a wide new dimension to the tactical employment of infantry.

With the gradual introduction of the flintlock in the late seventeenth century, more reliable by far than the smouldering match, the rate of fire of the infantry rose dramatically and three rounds a minute were common (some seasoned soldiers achieved five rounds a minute). Firepower had become a reality, with blistering volleys of highly disciplined musketry scouring the battlefield. The technique, in certain circumstances, of soldiers in rear ranks loading muskets and passing them to the front for the better shots to use was also not uncommon, increasing still further the rate of fire.

Rapidity of fire was one thing, but accuracy and effect was quite another. The muskets commonly in use at the time were, contrary to general belief, quite accurate to about 300 metres if used carefully. However, the smoke obscuration from the black powder used, and the heat and excitement of battle, hampered such use, and the temptation to load and loose the round off at the greatest rate, regardless of accuracy, is a problem experienced by commanders right down to the present day. Initially the soldiers, once drawn up in a series of ranks (usually five in the French army but three in English battalions, and subsequently those of her allies), would fire at the order of the company officers, a whole rank at a time – rear rank, second rank and so on. This was very difficult to control, especially as the soldiers tired and smoke gathered, and much of this fire was wasted. Accordingly, a new system was developed, and taught in the English army by, among others, John Churchill as early as the 1670s. The Dutch and Swedes did the same. This was known as 'platoon firing', and involved the thirteen platoons in a battalion firing in a well-ordered group sequence on the word of command. As a general rule the front rank would reserve its fire until the decisive moment, or when faced with a sudden threat, as with a rush of enemy cavalry. The weight of each volley was rather less than that produced when firing by rank, but it was more accurate and, given the number of combinations of platoons and the rate at which muskets were reloaded, the opposing troops were never free of the tormenting lash of musketry. The platoons on either flank of the battalion would incline inwards to envelope the opposing ranks with musketry, and soldiers were taught to concentrate their fire at the colour parties, the officers and the drummers, to disrupt the command and control arrangements of the enemy. So effective was the platoon firing system compared with volley firing by ranks, that the French army introduced the new system unofficially in 1708, although its use by their Bavarian allies is recorded as early as 1705.

Each infantry battalion fielded about 600 men at full strength (French battalions, as with the cavalry squadrons, were slightly smaller than their English and Dutch counterparts). Every battalion had a grenadier company, and these soldiers were generally taller and stronger than the ordinary infantryman. Often wearing tall conical hats (sometimes tipped with fur), the grenadiers carried the normal musket and sword, in addition to a long handled hatchet – a very useful tool when clearing obstacles. A number of grenades (iron bombs filled with gunpowder) would be carried in a pouch slung at the soldier's side, but the use of this weapon was diminishing by 1704, outside of entrenchments and houses where they would have most effect.

The use of small battalion guns was quite widespread. Pairs of these light pieces, two and three pounders, were attached to the infantry units and were mobile enough to be manhandled about the battlefield. Firing canister shot they could be quite effective at close range, although the crews, drawn for the men in the battalion, were an inviting target and were very vulnerable to enemy musketry.

The Artillery

Coehorn mortar, c.1704.

Field gun, c.1704.

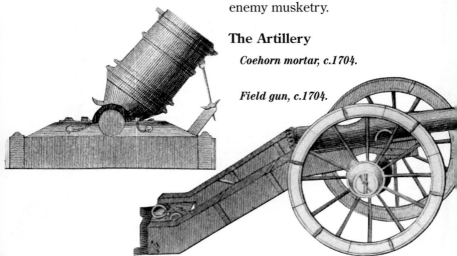

Siege artillery in action, c.1700. The lack of a proper siege train hampered Marlborough's operations in Bavaria.

The method of the tactical use of artillery in 1704 was that of a fairly static and cumbersome arm. The carriages of the guns were very heavy and the crews were often comprised of civilian contractors hired to serve for a certain period on campaign. They were well paid, and valued for their expertise, but their *ésprit de corps*, in general, was not likely to be highly developed, although the gunner officers were highly proficient professionals. Despite this, the civilian teamsters often displayed great bravery and devotion to the pieces they served.

The field artillery, guns firing nine, twelve, eighteen and twenty-four pound round-shot, were grouped into batteries each of six or eight pieces. The technique generally in use was to emplace the battery at some convenient spot on the field of battle, and then to fight the pieces from there, come what may, as the battle unfolded. The sheer weight of the guns did not encourage mobility in action. In addition, the tactics were not so developed as to facilitate much mobility, but this was largely a matter of customary practice. Against massed troops, this battering ram technique could be deadly. When occasion demanded, however, guns could be and were manhandled forward in action, to gain a better position or improved field of fire, and were fought close up to their opponents. Colonel Holcroft Blood did this at Blenheim where he got several batteries across the Nebel stream, at great effort, to engage the French infantry on the plain of Höchstädt. This was not all on one side; for the Marquis de la Frequelière, Tallard's artillery commander at Blenheim, earned great praise for the aggressive and imaginative handling of his batteries that day.

The guns fired iron round-shot at medium and long range, anything over about 200 metres. At closer range canister shot was used. This comprised tin cans of musket balls which, when fired from a gun, sprayed out viciously like a giant shotgun. The effect upon massed troops in the open, whether cavalry or infantry, could be dreadfully effective. This was also true against troops in light defences, for the breaching power of canister shot (and also grapeshot, although this was a naval weapon) at short range was very effective.

Sieges were a major part of warfare at this time, and large siege guns, and mortars heavy and immobile, were needed to reduce the defences of even such minor fortresses as Rain in Bavaria, which defied Marlborough for four days in July 1704. Howitzers and mortars (commonly called coehorns at this time), firing at a high angle, were routinely used at sieges and against buildings. They were also used on occasion against troops in the open. Firing an explosive shell (a hollow cannonball filled with gunpowder and sometimes musket balls), the ability of these weapons to search into dead ground and behind cover was a valuable asset to a commander. On the other hand, light and mobile horse artillery, galloper guns as they became known, were a species not yet developed and are not to be confused with battalion guns.

The supply of draught animals, horses and oxen was a constant concern, as is shown in the letters sent during the campaign. Marlborough wrote to his brother, Charles Churchill, on 1 June 1704 of the need to plan ahead and conserve the strength of the animals:

> *Pray acquaint Col. Blood that he should spare the contractor's horses as much as may be, and make use of as*

Nine-pounder field gun, c.1700.

> many others for the train as the country can afford even one
> march beyond *[*the pass at*] Gieslingen, after which he can
> expect no more assistance from the country, but must depend
> entirely on his own horses.*

To this must be added the difficulty in maintaining adequate
supplies of ammunition, roundshot and canister shot (rather
charmingly known by the English troops as 'partridge shot'),
powder, slow match and fodder for the horses and oxen. To move
a 'train' of artillery at all was an enormous logistical and
organisational feat, and the fact that the trains on campaign
covered such great distances says a lot for the expertise of the
gunner officers and their civilian teams. Progress could be slow,
with the heavy guns moving ponderously over bad roads. This
exerted a drag on the plans of commanding generals, sometimes
delaying the onset of battle, or causing an action to be undertaken
before the artillery was all in place, as with Eugene's attack on
Lutzingen.

The Engineers
The latter part of the seventeenth century had been an age of
great military engineers, such as the renowned French Marshal
Vauban and the Dutch general Coehorn, whose scientific

119

The running footmen

All commanding generals had a small staff whose primary task was to tour the battlefield gathering information or delivering messages and orders. Customarily these were noble or gently bred young men, sometimes volunteers and sometimes officers seconded from their regiment, placed in the entourage of a famous general to find advancement in the world. Mounted and conspicuous, they were easy to spot and rather vulnerable.

The Duke of Marlborough, in addition, developed a small corps of running footmen, whose task was close battlefield reconnaissance. Less conspicuous than staff officers, but distinctively clad in the Duke's livery, the footmen each carried a staff as a badge of office, topped with silver or gold depending on rank. Fit, agile and alert, these men had the licence to go wherever they could on the day of battle – they were immediately recognisable as the Duke's men, scouring the battlefield to observe with practised eyes what was going on, and then returning to the Duke with the vital information.

The flexible nature of the running footmen system enabled Marlborough to 'see over the other side of the hill' in a way that others could only do at a slower speed, if at all. The benefits that this important tactical advantage brought to the Duke's conduct of a battle are apparently evident. However, it also seems that the Duke was the only commander to use men on foot in this distinct way, so perhaps they were not as effective at intelligence gathering as is often thought.

methods of building very complex defences and fortresses were a feature of the campaigns of the latter part of the century. While fascinating in themselves, these fortresses and siege warfare generally played little part in the 1704 campaign in southern Germany and, accordingly, will not be explored further here.

There were no formed corps of Engineers at this time, but in all armies officers and NCOs who specialised in the art would receive additional pay and prerequisites. They would supervise squads of nominated soldiers, civilian contractors and impressed peasants in carrying out engineering tasks. As in the getting of volunteers for an assault, the prospect of extra money would usually induce soldiers to volunteer for these laborious duties readily enough. By 1704 most armies employed squads of specialist pioneers on road improvement duties, but paradoxically this vital role this was considered rather a low-grade duty, and disgraced soldiers were often designated to undertake pioneer tasks.

At a tactical level, mobility and counter-mobility, the never changing primary roles of the engineer services, were of particular importance in the Danube campaign. Roads at this time were generally bad, rutted and uneven, dusty in sunshine and muddy in rain. Engineers would prepare the route for an army, and remove obstacles, as an everyday task. The achievement of Tallard's engineers in bringing his army through the passes of the Black Forest, not once but twice in 1704, was notable. The many wide rivers in the region, such as the Danube and the smaller Lech, could provide considerable protection against an invading army, and if the few good crossing places were held in enough strength and in good time, an enemy might be turned away without fighting. The importance of the crossing places over the Danube at Donauwörth, the very reason why the desperate battle at the Schellenberg hill was fought, neatly illustrates this. Even such smaller rivers as the Wörnitz, across which Marlborough's army marched to that battle, required bridging. A fit man might (and in this case can) wade across, but an army with all its equipment could not do so in good order.

The engineer pontoon train, the 'tin boats' often referred to in accounts of the campaigns of this time, was an invaluable tool. Although cumbersome to move, the pontoons could be laid across quite wide rivers remarkably quickly and gave an army mobility. This ability to cross water obstacles, almost at will, removed the protection afforded by river lines to an opposing commander

The Duke of Marlborough at Blenheim.

Lt-Gen. William, Lord North and Grey. He lost his right hand at Blenheim, where he served on Marlborough's staff.

when on the back foot. The loss of the Bavarian pontoon train, abandoned at the edge of the Danube after the Schellenberg fight, was a severe loss to the Elector's ability to campaign fully. The withdrawal of the Bavarians and their French allies behind the Lech river after their defeat in early July afforded only a very temporary reprieve, with Marlborough's army breaking across

French troops on the march, c.1700.

the Danube and rampaging deep into Bavaria at will, courtesy of the Allied pontoon train. The Duke would undoubtedly have used the train to breach the line of the Lech in earnest, had Tallard not arrived with a fresh army from Alsace in the first week of August.

The staff

Considering the numerous tasks that an army commander has to perform – the planning of a campaign, the ordering of the stores, arranging orders of march for the troops, gathering intelligence of the enemy movements, co-ordinating operations with allies, and on the day of battle the drawing up into array of the army, considering enemy intentions, reconnaissance of the ground preparation and issuing of orders, control of movement under fire and many other simultaneous and demanding tasks, the very smallness of the size of the staff of commanding generals at this time is astonishing. Having such a small staff imposed tremendous demands upon a commanding general, who often had to turn aside from consideration of weighty matters to attend to quite minor things. During the pursuit of the broken French and Bavarian armies after Blenheim, little escaped Marlborough's keen eye, and on 25 August 1704 he wrote to a Colonel Herman:

> *When the artillery, which I have written to you about, is ready from Donauwörth, I wish you to arrange a Lieutenant and thirty men of your regiment to accompany them, to serve as escort on the road to Mayenne, where that Lieutenant will get orders to rejoin the regiment.*

Marlborough worked with a few close and trusted colleagues, issuing relatively few orders in writing but confident that they understood his method of campaigning, and would respond accordingly. The assistance of such a staunch lieutenant as William Cadogan, the Quartermaster-General of the Allied army, was an enormous benefit to the Duke on campaign, but the Duke regretted the loss at the Schellenberg fight of Johan Goor, whose efficient staff work had also been of great value. Life on the staff was no restful sinecure: the officers were conspicuously mounted and often in the most exposed spots. William, Lord North and Grey, whose regiment fought for the churchyard at Blindheim, lost his right hand in the battle, while serving as an aide to Marlborough.

The logistics of the campaign

The opposing armies in the Danube campaign managed their re-supply arrangements rather differently. Marlborough's preparations for the march up the Rhine were admirably complete, and he was able, once he passed into Swabia, to set new lines of supply and communication into central Germany, rather than along the vulnerable route all the way back to the Low Countries. Able to pay in hard cash, the Duke found that supplies for his troops were readily available. His Imperial allies were not in quite the same happy position and were short of money, and so often they depended upon Marlborough to re-supply them. This plainly imposed strain on the logistic arrangements made by the Duke, who was aware that both England and Holland had paid huge financial subsidies to the Emperor. These sums were, in fact, spent in quelling a rebellion in Hungary rather than supporting the campaign in Bavaria.

The Elector of Bavaria was operating in his own lands, and could levy supplies from his own populace. This he did ruthlessly, but the ability of the area to support both his army, and eventually two French armies (those of Marsin and Tallard) was a strain. Once the Allied army had ravaged Bavaria in July 1704 the Elector no longer had the ability to feed all his own troops, and the arrival of Tallard's column was as welcome for the supplies that the Marshal brought, as for the French troops that were added to the order of battle against Marlborough.

The French method of gathering supplies on campaign was a rough one. They took what they needed when and where they could. In part this was necessity, since the French treasury had not the power to dispense the vast sums that London and the Hague could summon to the support of their armies. Also, this method of confiscating supplies was not seen as unduly ruthless at the time, savage though it seems today. War was a tough matter and gathering supplies from the locals was just a part of the whole business. The disadvantage was that the locals would resist and hamper the French, as far as they were able, while they would welcome Marlborough's quartermasters, with their valuable ability to pay for what was taken.

To pay, feed, clothe, house and administer to the needs of an army was a complex undertaking on campaign, and in the aftermath of battle, particularly for the losers when all was in chaos, it could be a nightmarish task, if it was undertaken at all. Merode-Westerloo remembered finding some of his own wounded men on the retreat from the Danube:

> I came across a number of Spanish [Walloon or Flemish] officers from my cavalry in a penniless condition. They were doomed to stay in Ulm. It appeared that our pay office had no funds to deal with any unusual needs or accidents. So, poor though I was – with almost all my property confiscated – I had stretchers made for them, engaged good surgeons, had their soup and bread cooked in my kitchens and finally had them brought into the quarters assigned to me all the way to Strasbourg, whilst I myself lived in a tent.

The medical services
By modern standards the care of the sick and wounded of an army in 1704 seems ludicrously primitive, but the soldiers were a tough lot and few seemed to think the arrangements odd. Surprisingly many men (and a few women) suffered severe gunshot wounds and survived to tell the tale. Donald McBane, who fought in Orkney's Regiment at Blenheim, lay wounded on the trampled wheat for two days, and drank his own blood to slake his thirst in the hot August sun, before his friends found him and

Kneeling British grenadier, from the Blenheim Tapestry. By kind permission of His Grace the Duke of Marlborough.

took him to a surgeon. James Campbell wrote of a friend who was also wounded that day:

> *Willie Primrose is shoot through the bodie but we are hopeful he should recover. I have had a letter from him since which gives me good hopes of him he is very lustie.*

In Marlborough's army each regiment had a surgeon and surgeon's mate, and their apparently rough skills were put to good use during a battle and its aftermath. Similar arrangements were in place in all other armies, to a greater or lesser degree. The gathering in and care of the wounded after an engagement was a constant problem, and could be a rather makeshift affair – as McBane found. The day after the battle of Blenheim, one hundred men from each Allied battalion were detailed to scour the battlefield to bring in the wounded to the regimental surgeons; the Allied wounded that is, the French and Bavarians were left where they were. Parties of local peasants were detailed to gather and bury the dead, and they probably did a fair amount of plundering too.

On a larger scale, commanders usually made arrangements in advance for the reception and care of casualties in a forthcoming battle. Prior to the assault on the Schellenberg, Marlborough sent instructions to establish hospitals in Nordlingen. Dr Hare wrote:

> *He* [the Duke] *then sent an express to the commissary of the hospital to hasten him to Nordlingen, and to march day and night, till he had settled with it there. This express was followed by two more, to hasten the apothecaries and surgeons.*

The British Regiments in the 1704 Danube Campaign

HORSE AND DRAGOONS

Lumley's Regiment (3 squadrons) — *Lieutenant Colonel T. Crowther*

Wood's Regiment (2 squadrons) — *Lieutenant Colonel J. Featherstonehaugh*

Cadogan's Regiment (1 squadron) — *Major R. Napier*

Schomberg's Regiment (2 squadrons) — *Lieutenant Colonel C. De Sybourg*

Hay's Regiment of Dragoons (1 squadron) — *Lieutenant Colonel G. Preston*

Ross's Regiment of Irish Dragoons (3 squadrons) — *Lieutenant Colonel O. Wynne*

FOOT

1st Regiment of English Foot Guards — *Lieutenant Colonel P. Dormer/H Withers*

The Royal Regiment (Orkney's) (2 battalions) — *Earl Orkney/Major A. Hamilton*

Churchill's Regiment — *Lieutenant Colonel A. Peyton*

Webb's Regiment — *Lieutenant Colonel R. Sutton*

North & Grey's Regiment — *Lieutenant Colonel H. Groves*

Howe's Regiment — *Lieutenant Colonel W. Breton*

Earl of Derby's Regiment — *Lieutenant Colonel H. Hamilton*

Hamilton's Regiment — *Lieutenant Colonel R. Sterne*

Rowe's Regiment — *Lieutenant Colonel J. Dalyell*

Ingoldsby's Regiment of Fuzileers — *Lieutenant Colonel J. Sabine*

Duke of Marlborough's Regiment — *Lieutenant Colonel W. Tatton*

Ferguson's Regiment — *Lieutenant Colonel A. Livingston*

Meredith's Regiment — *Lieutenant Colonel T. Bellow*

The chain of command in the armies at Blenheim

THE ALLIED ARMY
Commanding General
The Duke of Marlborough

Left Wing				Right Wing
Marlborough			**Eugene**	
Churchill (Infantry)	Hesse-Cassell (Cavalry)	Hanover/Württemberg (Cavalry)		Anhalt-Dessau (Infantry)

THE FRANCO-BAVARIAN ARMIES

Left Wing				Right Wing
Elector of Bavaria/Marsin			**Tallard**	
Maffei/de Blainville (Infantry)	D'Arco/du Bourg (Cavalry)	von Zurlauben (Cavalry)		Clerambault (Infantry)

B. With no general in overall command, the co-ordination of the French and Bavarian rmies was inevitably less precise that that of the Allied army under Marlborough.

To aid in this work, the Duke also gave instructions that the 'widows' of the army (rather a euphemism to include those females who did not have actual marriage lines in their pockets) should report to Nordlingen to act as nurses to the wounded. Such was the scale of the fighting on the hill, that these makeshift hospitals were quite overwhelmed with numbers, and the magistrates of the town ordered that the more lightly wounded should be sent to outlying villages to ease the crowding.

Chapter 8

WALKING BLENHEIM BATTLEFIELD – A GUIDE

How to get there and where to stay

To drive from a Channel port allow two days. Flights to Munich can be found, via the internet, for £100 to £150 or less. It is advised that you arrange for a hire-car when you get there. Accommodation can be found at Ingolstadt at the Mercure Hotel (around £60 per person, per night) tel (+49) 8450/9220; e-mail H1974@accor-hotels.com. Or in Augsburg at the Ibis group (choice of two) (around £40) tel (+49) 821/50160 and (+49) 821/50310.

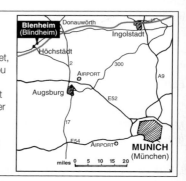

THE WIDE BAVARIAN CORNFIELDS of the Danube valley afford a magnificent setting as the scene of one of the greatest and most spectacular battles in history. Bounded on the southern side by the great river, and to the north by the wooded hills stretching to Swabia and Franconia, the battlefield at Blenheim is a delight to visit. Modern development has been quite limited and the small villages and hamlets, while rather larger than in 1704, are still distinct and have lost none of their charm and character. In fact, the houses today are unsurprisingly more prosperous in appearance than would have been the case 300 years ago, with the result that the villages are almost certainly more attractive now than when the armies of the Duke of Marlborough and Marshal Tallard met there.

The battlefield visitor to this beautiful area may wish to begin their tour at the attractive town of Donauwörth at the confluence of the Danube and Wörnitz rivers, only about fifteen minutes drive from the plain of Höchstädt itself. Looming over the old houses of Donauwörth is the Schellenberg, scene of the desperate assault on the entrenched French and Bavarians under Count D'Arco by Marlborough's advance guard, which took place on 2 July 1704. The actual scene of the action is separated from the fringes of the town by a modern bypass, and there is a public swimming pool in the trees near the crest of the hill, but much of the slope over which the troops fought with such ferocity is untouched. The rear of the slope, leading down towards the Danube, is now occupied by a German army base, and as a result is not open to the public. The wooded heights, however, give a wonderful view over the surrounding country, northwards to Ebermorgen, where the Allied armies crossed the old stone bridge over the Wörnitz river on their march to the Schellenberg, and westwards

130

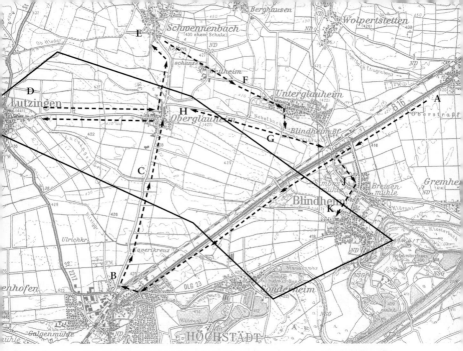

Map showing the walking tour, taken from Topographische Karte-Hochstadt a.d Danau 1:50,000 27328. The irregular shaped box marks the area over which the fighting took place.

up the line of the valley of the Danube, towards the plain of Höchstädt, the Nebel stream and Blindheim itself. If time allows, it is also well worthwhile to drive the twenty miles northwards to Nordlingen, the last completely walled town in Germany. The Allied wounded were brought here after both the Schellenberg fight and Blenheim; the Evangelische church contains a number of attractive and elaborate memorials to those senior officers who died. Among these is Marlborough's great friend, Johan Wigand van Goor, General of Dutch Infantry, who fell in the assault on the Schellenberg.

Taking the main road westwards, the B16 from Donauwörth towards Ulm, the villages of Münster and Tapfheim are soon reached. This is the route taken by Marlborough and Eugene, and is where the Allied armies combined on 11 August 1704, in the face of the threat of the advancing French and Bavarian forces. The distance between the river on the one hand and the wooded hills to the north makes this a vital narrow corridor for east-west movement, and it providentially offered a good position for defence, had the Duke and Eugene not had something far more adventurous in mind. In the village of Tapfheim, the two commanders climbed to the belfry of the ornate church tower to view 'through their perspective glasses' the growing encampment of the Elector and the Marshals on the plain of Höchstädt.

Just to the west of Tapfheim is the small village of Schwenningen, on the main B16 road, and nearby is the hamlet of Wolperstetten at the foot of the

131

Fuchsberg hill. The two Allied commanders rode into this area during 12 August 1704 to complete their close reconnaissance, and their cavalry escort clashed with French foragers while they did so. The Marquis de Silly sent his own cavalry forward to hamper the Allied pioneers as they laboured to clear paths for the army across the many small streams in the vicinity. The wooded hills beside the road sheltered the sleeping Allied army on the night before the battle.

At the scene of the great action itself, the B16 road runs straight across the Blenheim battlefield. It follows the ancient route, but it does not detract from the scene in any serious way. In the late nineteenth century a railway line was constructed next to the road but it follows the same course closely, although an embankment for the line is visible in a few places. Also, a road was recently (2001) built to bypass from north to south the village of Lutzingen, taking traffic from Höchstädt to Nordlingen, but it is not very obtrusive. On the southern and eastern edge of the battlefield, the river Danube has been channelled and straightened over the years, and no longer meanders through marshy meadows as in 1704. These meadows themselves have been largely drained, but are still wet underfoot in places, and the original course of river, rather like a shallow cutting, can be made out with careful observation.

The Nebel stream (shown on local maps as the Nebel Bach) is an obvious feature, splitting the battlefield in two as it crosses the plain from the hills to the north-west and running to a confluence with the Danube near to Blindheim. In most places the stream is about six to ten feet broad (narrower towards Lutzingen) and, although the ground is, as with the Danube, much better drained than in the past, the water is a very obvious obstacle to ease of movement. It is possible to scramble across, at the risk of a wetting (as the author has found) but this is neither easy nor recommended. Anyway, there are several farm track bridges which give easy passage these days. Some of these seem quite ancient and may well have been there at the time of the battle, to be partly demolished by the French and Bavarian picquets as they pulled back in the face of the Allied approach.

The ground between the Schwenningen defile and the Nebel stream, over which the Allied troops trudged into position that Sunday morning, is firm and obviously easy going. However, as the visitor moves past Unterglau towards Weilheim Farm and Schwennenbach, the area allotted to Prince Eugene in which to draw up his army, it is evident that the ground is less satisfactory and quite broken up in places. It is easy to see why, before modern drainage and land management techniques took effect, the Prince had such trouble getting his troops into place in good time. Also the topography of the area means that the ground close to the hills is, inevitably, slightly higher than that towards the Danube. Eugene's troops were in fact climbing a long, if quite gentle, incline to get into position.

After crossing the Nebel stream in the vicinity of Unterglau a short and easy slope (rising in all only from 415m elevation to 429m) leads a few hundred metres upwards to the plain of Höchstädt. This was the site of the encampment of the French and Bavarian armies. The open fields, often laid to wheat and oil-seed rape, and dotted with a few small copses of trees, provide

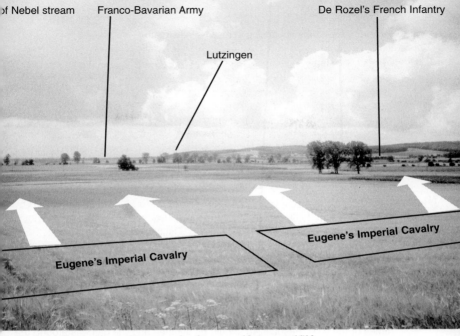

of Nebel stream   Franco-Bavarian Army   De Rozel's French Infantry

Lutzingen

Eugene's Imperial Cavalry

Eugene's Imperial Cavalry

Eugene attacked over this ground, afternoon 13 August 1704.

wide and attractive views in all directions, as Robert Parker said: 'Here was a fine plain for the cavalry on both sides to show their bravery.' There is hardly an obstacle to be seen, once the Nebel is crossed, and the whole arena of the vast conflict is laid open to the observer. The great distances involved – the field stretches for about four miles from Lutzingen to Blindheim, can be disconcerting at first. A few moments of orientation with map and compass is advisable. The hills of the Swabian Jura to the northwards are obvious, and the visitor will do well to pick out and identify the distinctive church towers in the villages – they can all be seen from virtually wherever you stand – Höchstädt, Blindheim, Schwenningen, Unterglau, Oberglau and Lutzingen. Identifying these and finding their location on a map provides both orientation and illustrates very well the great scale of the task for Tallard and his colleagues, when fighting a pitched battle under the hot August sun against an active and dangerous enemy. The failure of Tallard to appreciate sooner than he did what Clerambault was doing with the French infantry away on the right flank, becomes a little more understandable once you have see the expanse of the terrain, rather than simply reading the account on the page. In this way, Marlborough's overwhelming of the senses of the opposing commanders, with his fast-paced multiple attacks, can be seen to have worked its deadly effect.

When touring the Blenheim battlefield, it is best to take a modern map (Topographische Karte – Höchstädt a. d. Donau 1:50000 L7328) and compass, and binoculars. That much is obvious, and a well-drawn battle-plan to compare with the modern map will be useful. The ground is generally firm but

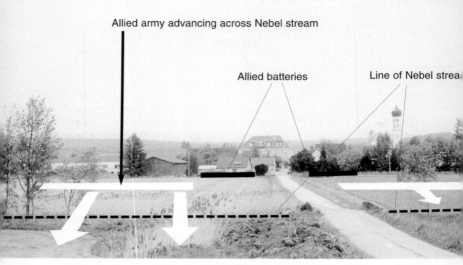

Allied army advancing across Nebel stream

Allied batteries

Line of Nebel stream

The village of Unterglau looking eastward across the stone bridge, believed to be the same as the one in 1704, over the Nebel stream.

stout shoes are advisable as the area along the Nebel is still muddy at certain times of the year. Trespassing should be avoided and the gardens around the villages are quite evidently private, but the author has found it possible to 'walk' pretty well the whole of the farmed parts of the battlefield. The country code should be used, as should common sense where crops are concerned, and a polite manner shown at all times. The sight of a stranger in walking boots poring over a map usually attracts a tolerant half-smile and a polite 'Gruss Gott' from local people.

The visitor may wish to start the tour of the ground at the roadside at Schwenningen (marked as Point A on the map on p131). Looking south-westwards across the open ground of the Oberstrassfeld towards Blindheim, the houses of which are partly hidden from view by trees, this is the scene that would have greeted Marlborough and his soldiers as they marched out onto the plain early in the morning of 13 August 1704. It is easy to appreciate just how narrow the gap is at Schwenningen and what a chance Tallard and his colleagues missed in not holding the place. It can also be seen what a difficult manoeuvre it was to thread the eight marching columns (nine if Cutts's column is counted) through the gap in good time and good order, before gaining the wider ground on which to form ready for battle.

From Schwenningen a short car drive down the main B16 road past Blindheim brings the visitor to Höchstädt. Turning sharp right at the entrance to the town on side road ST2383 leading to the ST2212 towards Lutzingen (Point B), the road leads gently upwards onto the plain of Höchstädt. Almost immediately after crossing the railway line turn right again onto a by-road, the DLG36 Glauheimerstrasse, towards Oberglau. Within half a mile, after passing a small crossroads known as the Xaverikreuz, you are among wide-open fields (Point C). Lutzingen is slightly to the left, Oberglau is straight ahead, Unterglau

134

is ahead and to the right beyond the line of small trees marking the course of the Nebel stream. Blindheim is off to the right. This is the site of the encampment of the French and Bavarian armies on the morning of 13 August 1704. Halting here and facing east, it is possible to view what the Comte de Merode-Westerloo and his comrades saw that daybreak, as the Allied armies poured forward through the Schwenningen defile into the open. On either side of the stream, beside Unterglau village, is the ground on which the Duke's army formed up, in full view of their enemies. Standing on the plain, it is immediately apparent what an advantage the French cavalry had, in being able to use the slope leading downwards to the stream, gradual though it is, when engaging Marlborough's advancing squadrons.

A short drive further along the DLG36 brings you to Oberglau, which the Marquis de Blainville and his French and émigré Irish infantry defended with such tenacity. There is not a lot to see in the village itself, so it is best to take the turning left along DLG38 to Lutzingen. On the forward edge of this village, near the junction with the route ST2212 which leads northwards through the Jura hills to Nordlingen, is the site of the Bavarian great battery, over which the Prussian infantry expended so much blood (Point D). There is little left of the gun emplacement – centuries of ploughing has seen to that, but it is easy to visualise the Bavarian gunners at their deadly work decimating the Prussian infantry as they pressed forward across the Nebel stream. Retracing steps to Oberglau, turn left across the Nebel to Schwennenbach (Point E). From the edge of the hamlet an excellent vista is obtained back towards the plain of Höchstädt. This is where Eugene struggled to get his army into position before lunch that day, and the wide open ground towards Lutzingen and Oberglau is that over which his desperately gallant attacks went in on Marsin and the Elector of Bavaria. From Schwennenbach drive along route DLG32 to Weilheim Farm (Point F). This sturdy group of buildings occupies a slight rise above the local fields and from the farm there is a fine field of view westwards to

Edge of Blindheim village looking north-west towards the plain of Höchstädt. Von Zurlauben's Gens D'Armes rode down Rowe's regiment in this area early afternoon, 13 August 1704.

ns D'Armes advance | Rowe's Regiment trying to form a square | Line of Nebel stream behind trees

Oberglau, Höchstädt and Lutzingen. Here Eugene placed his batteries rather late in the day, and it was across the wide cornfields ahead, beyond the Nebel stream, that his cavalry and infantry attacked Marshal Marsin and the Elector so devotedly and at such heavy cost, to physically fix their troops and mentally tie them down, and so prevent either commander from going to the assistance of Tallard closer to Blindheim. The course of the Nebel stream can be made out by the thin line of trees (partly demolished by local beavers) which crosses the entire frontage. There is little cover or dead ground to aid an attacker, as Eugene's troops found to their cost, and the French and Bavarian gunners had excellent fields of fire. It will be readily seen that the villages are set too far apart for the batteries sited there to support each other properly with overlapping fire.

Driving on to Unterglau, it is easy to park at the roadside in the village, and a short walk along one of the lanes between the houses, 500 metres or so, soon brings the visitor to the Nebel stream. There is a stone bridge almost opposite the church in Unterglau, and from here a good view westwards is gained of what the Allied soldiers saw as they crossed the stream to engage the French and Bavarians (Point G). Höchstädt church tower is straight ahead, almost beyond the brow of the plain, while that of Blindheim is to the left, partly hidden by trees. It will be seen that the slope, while gradual, puts part of the stream almost in dead ground to troops standing on the higher parts of the plain of Höchstädt. This posed a problem for the French gunners whose field of observation cannot have been good (the slope is rather less pronounced towards Lutzingen where the Bavarian artillery was placed). The wheat was unharvested on the day of the battle, and crops in the eighteenth century grew longer than they do today, so this would also have obscured lines of sight. Firing along the slope, rather than downwards to the stream, would have overcome the problem and this may explain why accounts of the French artillery effort to hamper Marlborough's deployment often mention the battery near to Blindheim as being most in action.

A few moments' walk takes the visitor up the short slope onto the plain of Höchstädt, where the Allied infantry and cavalry deployed after crossing the Nebel. With the stream at your back, Höchstädt church tower is more easily visible from here, dead ahead. It will immediately be noticed how the French artillery in Oberglau, off to the right, had no chance of achieving overlapping fire with the batteries in Blindheim to the left. As Captain Robert Parker wrote, the open fields all around provided a superb platform for 'the cavalry of both sides to show their bravery.'

From Unterglau, a short walk northwards along the Nebel stream brings the battlefield visitor to the strip of land between the village of Oberglau and the stream (Point H), where the Marquis de Blainville's French and Irish troops put in their shattering counter-attack against the Dutch infantry under the Prince of Holstein-Beck. The ground is still quite wet underfoot in places, and it is easy to imagine the Dutch soldiers floundering about in the mud, caught under the lash of de Blainville's musketry while Marshal Marsin's French cavalry came sweeping forward to destroy them. Looking to the north-east, Weilheim Farm can be clearly seen, and here Fugger's armoured cuirassiers stood, sternly refusing to move to the aid of the stricken Dutch, until called forward by Marlborough.

Finally, it is worth either walking along the bank of the Nebel stream (an under-pass gives the pedestrian a way across the railway line but care should be taken when crossing the main B16 Donauwörth-Ulm road) or driving the short distance along the DLG32 past the small railway station into Blindheim village itself. Here the dramatic climax to the day took place. The Nebel near the village is divided into two by a small tree-covered islet, and the banks of the stream, fringed here with willow trees, are still wet underfoot (Point J). The two water mills set alight by the French were sited here, by the road-bridge across the stream which takes the DLG22 into the centre of the village. It is not difficult to make out where Cutts's infantry lay while waiting for the order to assault the French barricades. Standing with your back to the Nebel and looking down the main street towards the church, the first turning on the right, a small residential road, brings you to an easy slope leading down from the plain of Höchstädt. Across this field swept von Zurlauben's Gens d'Armes to scatter Rowe's regiment in the opening moments of the battle. The lower lying ground along the bank of the stream sheltered Wilkes's Hessian brigade from French artillery fire, as the German troops moved into position once the Allied attack began, until they moved forward to recover Rowe's colours from the French cavalry.

The village contains a number of houses and barns, which are contemporary to the battle, and it will be seen that these are lower and smaller than the more modern, but very attractive, houses that comprise most of Blindheim today. Large parts of the place were devastated by fire during the

Looking westwards towards Höchstädt from the Nebel stream, Blindheim church tower is on the left through the trees. Photo taken from Point G.

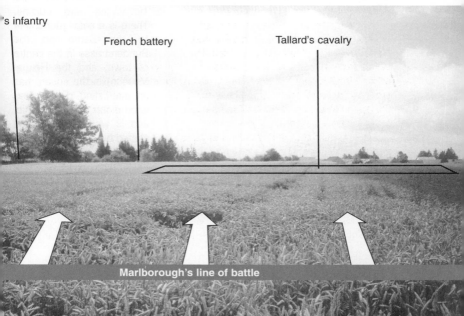

fighting of course, but the character of the village has not been lost over the years. Several of these old buildings, both cottages and barns, stand just across the road from the village church, and it is possible to make out the marks of musket balls in the walls, on close inspection. In the square stands the Baroque-style church (Point K). The interior is very attractive in an ornate way, but the visitor will find the walled churchyard of most interest. This was prepared for defence and held in strength by the French infantry in 1704, and a costly and bitterly contested battle at bayonet point was fought here in the closing moments of daylight. Orkney's infantry, deployed from the plain of Höchstädt to finish things, fought their bloody way along the street leading at right-angles along the churchyard wall to the main road through the village. Here in the square de Blanzac gave the dread order to the French regiments to lay down their arms and surrender their colours. Here too James Abercrombie tried to seize the regimental colour of the Régiment du Roi, and got cut across the forearm for his trouble. Set into the wall of the churchyard is a small commemorative plaque to the battle, but there are few other memorials or monuments to the great conflict in 1704. However, in 1997 a cap-badge of the Bedfordshire & Hertfordshire Regiment, whose predecessor unit, North and Grey's Regiment, fought here, was buried in a quiet corner of the much fought over churchyard. North and Grey's hold the ground still.

On leaving Blindheim village, take the road sign-posted to Höchstädt. Within about two kilometres the small hamlet of Sonderheim is reached, close to the original course of the Danube, where the fleeing French cavalry fell down the steep bank, as it was at the time. The river itself is now straightened and the marshy meadows are mostly drained. Near here Hessian dragoons confronted Marshal Tallard as he attempted to escape the rout of his army.

Finally, Höchstädt is a very pleasant small town, with a number of excellent bars and restaurants in which the weary battlefield traveller can refresh themselves with the local beverages and cuisine. There is a small monument to the battle on the Bunderstrasse in the centre of town, and the Heimat Museum in the square has an interesting display and large diorama of the battle, and is worth a visit. It is staffed by volunteers, and is open each first Sunday in the month, between 2 and 5pm. The museum address is: Alten Rathaus, Marktplatz 7, Höchstädt a. d. Donau.

Plaque set in Blindheim churchyard wall.

Seventeenth and eighteenth-century houses next to the churchyard in Blindheim village.

The plain of Höchstädt from the vicinity of Weilheim Farm, looking westwards to Lutzingen, with the author.

AM 13 AUGUST 1704
STANDEN IN DER SCHLACHT VON
HÖCHSTÄDT-BLINDHEIM IN EI-
NEM ENTSCHEIDENDEN RINGEN DES SPA-
NISCHEN ERBFOLGEKRIEGES DIE STREIT-
KRÄFTE DES KURFÜRSTEN MAX EMANUEL
UND DIE TRUPPEN LUDWIGS XIV UNTER
MARSCHALL TALLARD DEM KAISERLICHEN
HEER UNTER PRINZ EUGEN UND DEN
VERBUNDETEN DES KAISERS UNTER
DEM HERZOG MARLBOROUGH
GEGENÜBER

ERRICHTET 1954
IM GEDENKEN
AN DIE GEFAL-
LENEN ALLER
BETEILIGTEN
VÖLKER

AMOR
PAX
VITA
ODIUM
BELLUM
MORS

ÜBERWINDET
DEN HASS
SUCHET DEN
FRIEDEN

The two sides of the Höchstädt town memorial.

140

BIBLIOGRAPHY

The lively journals relating to the 1704 campaign that are available today make very entertaining reading. Two good accounts in a single volume, *Military Memoirs – The Marlborough's Wars*, can hardly be bettered for their entertaining details of campaign life on both sides of the military divide. This work, the memoirs of two valiant old soldiers, Captain Robert Parker and the Comte de Merode-Westerloo, was republished in 1998 by Greenhill Books. The Society of Army Historical Research has published the *Journal of John Deane*, an educated man who soldiered with the 1st English Foot Guards, and fought at both the Schellenberg and Blenheim. The career of James Campbell (Royal Scots Fusiliers and Royal Scots Greys) is well set out in Burn's edited account for the Society of Army Historical Research, *A Scots Fusilier and Dragoon Under Marlborough*. Mrs Christian Davies's extraordinary life as a woman soldier is amusingly told in Defoe's account of her career, related to him before her death and to be found in *Life and Adventures of Mother Ross*. Colonel De La Colonie left a graphic memoir of the desperate fighting of his regiment on the Schellenberg, in Horsley's edited account in *The Chronicles of an Old Campaigner*. However, he missed the battle of Blenheim as his unit was under siege by Baden in Ingolstadt. Finally, the *Letters and Dispatches of the Duke of Marlborough*, edited by General Murray in the 1840s, are indispensable and an absolute mine of primary source information. However, these volumes are rather difficult to find.

Contemporary sources
Black, J, *John Creed's letter from Blenheim*, Journal of Society of Army Historical Research 1986
Burn W L, *A Scots Fusilier and Dragoon Under Marlborough*, JSAHR, 1936
Chandler, D, (ed) *Military Memoirs – The Marlborough Wars*, 1968
Deane, J, *Journal of Marlborough's Campaigns* (ed D Chandler), JSAHR, 1984
Defoe, D, *Life and Adventures of Mother Ross (also known as Christian Davies)*, 1929 (ed J.Fortescue)
De La Colonie, J, *Chronicles of an Old Campaigner*, 1904 (ed W Horsley)
Hamilton, G, *Letters of 1st Earl Orkney*, English Historical Review, 1904
Noyes, S, *Letters*, JSAHR 1959 (ed S. Johnson)
Merode-Westerloo, E.J.P, *Mémoires,* 1840
Murray, G, (ed) *Letters and Dispatches of Marlborough*, 1845
Parker, R, *Memoirs,* 1747
Secondary sources
Chandler, D, *The Art of Warfare in the Age of Marlborough*, 1975
Churchill, W S, *Life and Times of Marlborough*, 1948
Coxe, W, *Memoirs of the Duke of Marlborough*, 1847
Donauwörth Stadt Archiv *Die Schlacten auf dem Schellenberg und bei Blindheim Höchstädt*, 1704
Falkner, J, *Great and Glorious Days*, 2002
　　　　　　The Schellenberg 1704, Battlefields Review, 1999
　　　　　　The Battle of Blenheim 1704, Battlefields Review, 2000
Fortescue, J, *History of the British Army, Vol I*, 1899
Green, D, *Blenheim*, 1977
Henderson, N, *Prince Eugen of Savoy*, 1964
Lediard, T, *Life of the Duke of Marlborough*, 1736
Phelan, I, *Marlborough as Logistician*, JSAHR 1989
Taylor, F, *The Wars of Marlborough*, 1921
Trevelyan, G M, *England Under Queen Anne – Blenheim*, 1933
Verney, P, *Blenheim*, 1975

INDEX